WHAT EVERY STUDENT SHOULD KNOW ABOUT WRITING ABOUT LITERATURE

Edgar V. Roberts

Lehman College
The City University of New York

Pearson

Boston   Columbus   Indianapolis   New York   San Francisco   Upper Saddle River
Amsterdam   Cape Town   Dubai   London   Madrid   Milan   Munich   Paris   Montreal   Toronto
Delhi   Mexico City   Sao Paulo   Sydney   Hong Kong   Seoul   Singapore   Taipei   Tokyo

Editor-in-Chief: Joseph Terry
Associate Development Editor: Erin Reilly
Executive Marketing Manager: Joyce Nilsen
Senior Supplements Editor: Donna Campion
Production Manager: Donna DeBenedictis
Project Coordination, Text Design, and Electronic Page Makeup: Grapevine Publishing
    Services, Inc.
Copyeditor: Leslie Ballard
Senior Designer: Sue Kinney
Senior Manufacturing Buyer: Roy Pickering
Printer and Binder: Edwards Brothers Malloy
Cover Printer: Edwards Brothers Malloy

Please visit us at www.pearsonhighered.com

3 4 5 6 7 8 9 10 — V069 — 14 13 12

ISBN 13: 978-0-205-23655-8
ISBN 10:   0-205-23655-3

www.pearsonhighered.com

CONTENTS

CHAPTER 1: *What Is Literature and Why Do We Study It?* **1**

Types of Literature   2

CHAPTER 2: *Reading Literature and Responding to It Actively* **5**

⌐ *Guy de Maupassant, The Necklace*   5

Reading and Responding in a Computer File or Notebook   14

Guidelines for Reading: Preparation for Writing   14

⌐ Sample Notebook or Journal Entries on Maupassant's "The Necklace"   16

CHAPTER 3: *Discovering Ideas*   **19**

The Goal of Writing: To Show a Process of Thought   19

Discovering Ideas ("Brainstorming")   22

Study the Characters in the Work   22

Determine the Work's Historical Period and Background   24

Analyze the Work's Economic and Social Conditions   24

Explain the Work's Major Ideas   25

Describe the Work's Artistic Qualities   26

Explain Any Other Approaches That Seem Important   27

CHAPTER 4: *Preparing to Write*   **28**

Build Ideas from Your Original Notes   28

Trace Patterns of Action and Thought   29

Raise and Answer Your Own Questions   30

Put Ideas Together Using a Plus-Minus, Pro-Con, or Either-Or Method   31

Originate and Develop Your Thoughts Through Writing   32

CHAPTER 5: *Make an Initial Draft of Your Essay*   **34**

Base Your Essay on a Central Idea, Argument, or Statement   34

Create a Thesis Sentence as Your Guide to Organization   36

⌐ The Need for a Sound Argument in Writing about Literature   37

Begin Each Paragraph with a Topic Sentence   38

Use Your Topic Sentences as Arguments for Your Paragraph
Development   38

   ⌐Referring to the Names of Authors   39

Select Only One Topic—No More—for Each Paragraph   40

Develop an Outline as the Means of Organizing Your Essay   40

Use Your Outline When Developing Your Essay   42

   ⌐Illustrative Essay (First Draft)   42

**CHAPTER 6: *Completing the Essay: Developing and
         Strengthening Your Ideas Through
         Revision   45***

Make Your Own Arrangement of Details and Ideas   45

Use Details from the Work as Evidence to Support Your
Argument   46

Always Keep to Your Point; Stick to It Tenaciously   48

Try to Be Original   50

Write with Specific Readers as Your Intended Audience   51

   ⌐The Use of Verb Tenses in the Discussion
      of Literary Works   52

Use Exact, Comprehensive, and Forceful Language   53

   ⌐Illustrative Essay (Improved Draft)   56

   ⌐A Summary of Guidelines   62

**CHAPTER 7: *A Short Guide to Using Quotations
         and Making References in Essays about
         Literature   63***

Integrate Passages and Ideas into Your Essay   63

Distinguish Your Own Thoughts from Those of Your
Author   63

Integrate Material by Using Quotation Marks   64

Blend Quotations into Your Own Sentences   66

Indenting and Blocking Long Quotations   66

Use Ellipses to Show Omissions   68

Use Square Brackets to Enclose Words That You Add within
Quotations   69

Do Not Overquote   69

APPENDIX: *Documenting Your Work in MLA Style   70*

1

WHAT IS LITERATURE AND WHY DO WE STUDY IT?

The objective in writing about literature is really the same as the objective in all the writing assignments for any of your courses. The point is that no educational process is complete until you can *apply* what you study. That is, you have not learned something—really *learned* it—until you can, first of all, *think* about it, and then *talk or write* about it convincingly. Your goal is to persuade your readers that your perceptions are accurate, your ideas are reliable, and your mind is strong.

This does not mean that you retell a story, state an undeveloped opinion, or describe no more than an author's life, but rather that you deal directly with topical and artistic issues about individual stories, poems, and plays. Your writing assignment requires that you strengthen your understanding and knowledge through the recognition of where your original study of the reading might have fallen short. Thus, it is easy for you to read a story like Guy de Maupassant's "The Necklace" (see p. 5) and follow the major events, right to the conclusion. But if you have been assigned to describe the *reasons* that Maupassant's principal character, Mathilde Loisel, borrows a necklace from her friend, you have left the arena of describing events, and are now drawing conclusions about the reasons for Mathilde's actions. It is not enough, in other words, to state simply that she borrows the necklace, but instead it is necessary to consider the underlying reasons for which she believes it necessary to borrow the necklace at all.

This is typical of the sort of writing assignment you may expect in courses requiring the examination and discussion of literature. You will need to develop a method for considering literature, just as you do when following methods in other courses, such as physics, chemistry, political science, history, psychology, or medicine. When you study literature, you will need to reread parts of the work, study your notes, and apply your knowledge to the problem at hand; you must check facts, grasp relationships, develop insights, and try to express yourself with as much certainty and exactness as possible. Your assignment topics may include: the analysis of a particular character in a story or play; the organization or structure of a poem; the symbolism in a poem or story; a comparison of two different poems or stories; the nature of a particular character's speeches in a story or play; an analysis of a special problem that might arise concerning a character's actions in a story, poem, or play; a poet's choice of words, his or her expressions about the natural world or locations where major characters live; and so on.

Primarily, then, you will need to improve your analytical and writing skills through the use of literature as subject matter. After you have finished a number of paragraphs, tests, and essays on literary topics, you will be able to approach just about any literary work with the confidence that you can understand it and write about it.

Types of Literature

The types of literature about which you will be asked to write may be conveniently considered as four categories or *genres:* (1) prose fiction, (2) poetry, (3) drama, and (4) nonfiction prose. Usually the first three are classified as *imaginative literature.* The genres of imaginative literature have much in common, but they also have distinguishing characteristics. *Prose fiction,* or *narrative fiction,* includes *myths, parables, romances, novels,* and *short stories.* Originally, *fiction* meant anything made up, crafted, or shaped, but today the word refers to prose stories based in the imaginations of authors. The essence of fiction is *narration,* the relating or recounting of a sequence of events or actions to one or more major characters who change and grow as they interact with other characters and situations, and as they attempt to solve the various problems they face. These characters may develop in terms of their awareness or insight, their intellect, their attitude toward others, their sensitivity, their moral capacity, and their ability to make decisions. Although fiction, like all imaginative literature, can introduce true historical details, it is not real history, for its main purpose is to interest, stimulate, instruct, and divert—not to create a precise historical record.

If prose is expansive, *poetry* tends toward brevity. It offers us high points of emotion, reflection, thought, and feeling in what the English poet William Wordsworth (1770–1850) called "narrow room[s]." Yet, in this context, it expresses the most powerful and deeply felt experiences of human beings, often awakening deep responses of welcome recognition in readers: "Yes, I know what that's like. I would feel the same way. That's exactly right." Poems make us think, make us reflect, and generally instruct us. They can also stimulate us, surprise us, make us laugh or cry, inspire us, exalt us. Many poems become our lifelong friends, and we visit them again and again for insight, understanding, laughter, or the quiet reflection of joy or sorrow.

The power of poetry lies not only in its words and thoughts, but also in its verbal music, using a variety of *rhythms*, and often *rhymes*, to intensify its emotional impact. Although poems themselves vary widely in length, individual lines are often short because poets aim at evoking the greatest meaning and imaginative power from their words through rhetorical devices such as *imagery* and *metaphor*. Important poetic forms include the fourteen-line *sonnet*, as well as *ballads*, *blank verse*, *couplets*, *elegies*, *epigrams*, *hymns*, *limericks*, *odes*, *quatrains*, *songs* or *lyrics*, *tercets* or *triplets*, *jingles*, *villanelles*, and the increasingly popular *haiku*. Many songs or lyrics have been set to music, and some were written expressly for that purpose. Some poems are long and discursive, like many poems by the American poet Walt Whitman. *Epic poems*, such as those by the ancient Greek Homer and the seventeenth-century Englishman John Milton, often contain thousands of lines. Since the time of Whitman, many poets have abandoned rhymes and regular rhythms in favor of *free verse*, a far-ranging type of poetry growing out of content and the natural rhythms of spoken language.

Drama is literature designed for stage or film presentation by people—actors—for the benefit and delight of other people—an audience. The essence of drama is the development of character and situation through speech and action. Like fiction, drama may focus on a single character or a small number of characters, and it enacts fictional (and sometimes historical) events as if they were happening right before our eyes. The audience therefore is a direct witness to the ways in which characters are influenced and changed by events, and by other characters. Although most modern plays use *prose dialogue* (the conversation of two or more characters), on the principle that the language of drama should resemble the language of ordinary people as much as possible, many plays from the past, such as those of ancient Greece and Renaissance England, are in poetic form.

Nonfiction prose consists of news reports, feature articles, essays, scientific reports, editorials, textbooks, historical and biographical works, and the like, all of which describe or interpret facts and present judgments and opinions. The goal of nonfiction prose is to present truths and conclusions about the factual world. Imaginative literature, although also grounded in facts, is less concerned with the factual record than with the revelation of truths about life and human nature. Recently, another genre has been emphasized within the category of nonfiction prose—*creative nonfiction*, a type of literature that is technically nonfiction, such as essays, articles, diaries, and journals, but that nevertheless introduces carefully structured form, vivid examples, relevant quotations, and highly creative and imaginative insights.

2

READING LITERATURE AND RESPONDING TO IT ACTIVELY

Sometimes, after we have finished reading a work, we find it difficult to express our thoughts and answer pointed questions about it. But more active and thoughtful reading gives us the understanding to develop well-considered answers. Obviously, we need to follow the work and understand its details, but just as importantly, we need to respond to the words, get at the ideas, and understand all of the implications. We rely on our own fund of knowledge and experience to verify the accuracy and truth of events, and we try to articulate our own emotional responses to the characters and their problems.

To illustrate such active responding, we will examine "The Necklace" (1884), by the French writer Guy de Maupassant. "The Necklace" is one of the best known of all stories written during the last century and a half, and it is included here in full.

Guy de Maupassant (1850–1893)
The Necklace

Translated by Edgar V. Roberts

She was one of those pretty and charming women, born, as if by an error of destiny, into a family of clerks and copyists. She had no dowry, no prospects, no way of getting known, courted, loved, married by a rich and distinguished man. She finally settled for a marriage with a minor clerk in the Ministry of Education.

She was a simple person, without the money to dress well, but she was as unhappy as if she had gone through bankruptcy, for women have neither rank nor race. In place of high birth or important family connections, they can rely only on their beauty, their grace, and their charm. Their inborn finesse, their elegant taste, their engaging personalities, which are their only power, make working-class women the equals of the grandest ladies.

She suffered constantly, feeling herself destined for all delicacies and luxuries. She suffered because of her grim apartment with its drab walls, threadbare furniture, ugly curtains. All such things, which most other women in her situation would not even have noticed, tortured her and filled her with despair. The sight of the young country girl who did her simple housework awakened in her only a sense of desolation and lost hopes. She daydreamed of large, silent anterooms, decorated with oriental tapestries and lighted by high bronze floor lamps, with two elegant valets in short culottes dozing in large armchairs under the effects of forced-air heaters. She imagined large drawing rooms draped in the most expensive silks, with fine end tables on which were placed knick-knacks of inestimable value. She dreamed of the perfume of dainty private rooms, which were designed only for intimate tête-à-têtes with the closest friends, who, because of their achievements and fame, would make her the envy of all other women.

When she sat down to dinner at her round little table covered with a cloth that had not been washed for three days, in front of her husband who opened the kettle while declaring ecstatically, "Ah, good old beef stew! I don't know anything better," she dreamed of expensive banquets with shining place settings, and wall hangings portraying ancient heroes and exotic birds in an enchanted forest. She imagined a gourmet-prepared main course carried on the most exquisite trays and served on the most beautiful dishes, with whispered gallantries that she would hear with a sphinxlike smile as she dined on the pink meat of a trout or the delicate wing of a quail.

5   She had no decent dresses, no jewels, nothing. And she loved nothing but these; she believed herself born only for these. She burned with the desire to please, to be envied, to be attractive, and to be sought after.

She had a rich friend, a comrade from convent days, whom she did not want to see anymore because she suffered so much when she returned home. She would weep for the entire day afterward with sorrow, regret, despair, and misery.

Well, one evening, her husband came home glowing and carrying a large envelope.

"Here," he said, "this is something for you."

She quickly tore open the envelope and took out a card engraved with these words:

> *The Chancellor of Education and Mrs. George Ramponneau*
> *request that Mr. and Mrs. Loisel do them the honor of*
> *coming to dinner at the Ministry of Education on the*
> *evening of January 8.*

10   Instead of being delighted, as her husband had hoped, she threw the invitation spitefully on the table, muttering:

"What do you expect me to do with this?"

"But Sweetie, I thought you'd be glad. You never get to go out, and this is a special occasion! I had a lot of trouble getting the invitation. The demand is high and not many clerks get invited. Everyone important will be there."

She looked at him angrily and stated impatiently:

"What do you expect me to wear to go there?"

15   He had not thought of that. He stammered:

"But your theater dress. That seems nice to me . . ."

He stopped, amazed and bewildered, as his wife began to cry. Large tears fell slowly from the corners of her eyes to her mouth. He said falteringly:

"What's wrong? What's the matter?"

But with a strong effort she had recovered, and she answered calmly as she wiped her damp cheeks:

20   "Nothing, except that I have nothing to wear and therefore can't go to the party. Give your invitation to someone else at the office whose wife will have nicer clothes than mine."

Distressed, he responded:

"Well, all right, Mathilde. How much would a new dress cost, something you could use at other times, but not anything fancy?"

She thought for a few moments, adding things up and thinking also of an amount that she could ask without getting an immediate refusal and a frightened outcry from the frugal clerk.

Finally she responded tentatively:

25 "I don't know exactly, but it seems to me that I could get by on four hundred francs."

He blanched slightly at this, because he had set aside just that amount to buy a shotgun for Sunday lark-hunts the next summer with a few friends in the Plain of Nanterre.

However, he said:

"All right, you've got four hundred francs, but make it a pretty dress."

As the day of the party drew near, Mrs. Loisel seemed sad, uneasy, anxious, even though her gown was all ready. One evening her husband said to her:

30 "What's the matter? You've been acting funny for several days."

She answered:

"It's awful, but I don't have any jewels to wear, not a single gem, nothing to dress up my outfit. I'll look like a beggar. I'd almost rather not go to the party."

He responded:

"You can wear a corsage of cut flowers. This year it's all the rage. For only ten francs you can get two or three gorgeous roses."

35 She was not convinced.

"No . . . there's nothing more humiliating than looking shabby in the company of rich women."

But her husband exclaimed:

"God, but you're silly! Go to your friend Mrs. Forrestier, and ask her to lend you some jewelry. You know her well enough to do that."

She uttered a cry of joy:

40 "That's right. I hadn't thought of that."

The next day she went to her friend's house and described her problem.

Mrs. Forrestier went to her mirrored wardrobe, took out a large jewel box, opened it, and said to Mrs. Loisel:

"Choose, my dear."

She saw bracelets, then a pearl necklace, then a Venetian cross of finely worked gold and gems. She tried on the jewelry in front of a mirror, and hesitated, unable to make up her mind about each one. She kept asking:

45 "Do you have anything else?"

"Certainly. Look to your heart's content. I don't know what you'd like best."

Suddenly she found a superb diamond necklace in a black satin box, and her heart throbbed with desire for it. Her hands shook as she picked it up. She fastened it around her neck, watched it gleam at her throat, and looked at herself ecstatically.

Then she asked, haltingly and anxiously:

"Could you lend me this, nothing but this?"

50 "Why yes, certainly."

She jumped up, hugged her friend joyfully, and then hurried away with her treasure.

The day of the party came. Mrs. Loisel was a success. She was prettier than anyone else, stylish, graceful, smiling and wild with joy. All the men saw her, asked her name, sought to be introduced. All the important administrators stood in line to waltz with her. The Chancellor himself eyed her.

She danced joyfully, passionately, intoxicated with pleasure, thinking of nothing but the moment, in the triumph of her beauty, in the glory of her success, on Cloud Nine with happiness made up of all the admiration, of all the aroused desire, of this victory so complete and so sweet to the heart of any woman.

She did not leave until four o'clock in the morning. Her husband, since midnight, had been sleeping in a little empty room with three other men whose wives had also been enjoying themselves.

55 He threw, over her shoulders, the shawl that he had brought for the trip home—a modest everyday wrap, the poverty of which contrasted sharply with the elegance of her evening gown. She felt it and hurried away to avoid being noticed by the other women who luxuriated in rich furs.

Loisel tried to hold her back:

"Wait a minute. You'll catch cold outdoors. I'll call a cab."

But she paid no attention and hurried down the stairs. When they reached the street they found no carriages. They began to look for one, shouting at cabmen passing by at a distance.

They walked toward the Seine, desperate, shivering. Finally, on a quay, they found one of those old night-going buggies that are seen in Paris only after dark, as if they were ashamed of their wretched appearance in daylight.

60   It took them to their door, on the Street of Martyrs, and they sadly climbed the stairs to their flat. For her, it was finished. As for him, he could think only that he had to begin work at the Ministry of Education at ten o'clock.

She took the shawl off her shoulders, in front of the mirror, to see herself once more in her glory. But suddenly she cried out. The necklace was no longer around her neck!

Her husband, already half undressed, asked:

"What's wrong?"

She turned toward him frantically:

65   "I . . . I . . . I no longer have Mrs. Forrestier's necklace."

He stood up, bewildered:

"What! . . . How! . . . It's not possible!"

And they looked in the folds of the gown, in the folds of the shawl, in the pockets, everywhere. They found nothing.

He asked:

70   "You're sure you still had it when you left the party?"

"Yes. I checked it in the vestibule of the Ministry."

"But if you'd lost it in the street, we would've heard it fall. It must be in the cab."

"Yes, probably. Did you notice the number?"

"No. Did you see it?"

75   "No."

Overwhelmed, they looked at each other. Finally, Loisel got dressed again:

"I'm going out to retrace all our steps," he said, "to see if I can find the necklace that way."

And he went out. She stayed in her evening dress, without the energy to get ready for bed, stretched out in a chair, drained of strength and thought.

Her husband came back at about seven o'clock. He had found nothing.

80   He went to Police Headquarters and to the newspapers to announce a reward. He went to the small cab companies, and finally he followed up even the slightest hopeful lead.

She waited the entire day, in the same enervated state, in the face of this frightful disaster.

Loisel came back in the evening, his face pale and haggard. He had found nothing.

"You'll have to write to your friend," he said, "that you broke a clasp on her necklace and that you're having it fixed. That'll give us time to look around."

She wrote as he dictated.

85   By the end of the week they had lost all hope.

And Loisel, looking five years older, declared:

"We'll have to see about replacing the jewels."

The next day they took the case that had contained the necklace and went to the jeweler whose name was inside. He looked at his books:

"I wasn't the one, Madam, who sold the necklace. I only made the case."

90   Then they went from jeweler to jeweler, searching for a necklace like the other one, racking their memories, both of them sick with worry and anguish.

In a shop in the Palais-Royal, they found a necklace of diamonds that seemed to them exactly like the one they were looking for. It was priced at forty thousand francs. They could buy it for thirty-six thousand.

They got the jeweler to promise not to sell it for three days. And they made an agreement that he would buy it back for thirty-four thousand francs if the original were recovered before the end of February.

Loisel had saved eighteen thousand francs that his father had left him. He would have to borrow the rest.

He borrowed, asking a thousand francs from one, five hundred from another, five louis* here, three louis there. He wrote

---

*louis: a gold coin worth twenty francs.

promissory notes, undertook ruinous obligations, did business with finance companies and the whole tribe of loan sharks. He compromised himself for the remainder of his days, risked his signature without knowing whether he would be able to honor it; and, terrified by anguish over the future, by the black misery that was about to descend on him, by the prospect of all kinds of physical deprivations and moral tortures, he went to get the new necklace, and put down thirty-six thousand francs on the jeweler's counter.

95 Mrs. Loisel took the necklace back to Mrs. Forrestier, who said with an offended tone:

"You should have brought it back sooner; I might have needed it."

She did not open the case, as her friend feared she might. If she had noticed the substitution, what would she have thought? What would she have said? Would she not have taken her for a thief?

Mrs. Loisel soon discovered the horrible life of the needy. She did her share, however, completely, heroically. That horrifying debt had to be paid. She would pay. They dismissed the maid; they changed their address; they rented an attic flat.

She learned to do the heavy housework, dirty kitchen jobs. She washed the dishes, wearing away her manicured fingernails on greasy pots and encrusted baking dishes. She handwashed dirty linen, shirts, and dish towels that she hung out on the line to dry. Each morning, she took the garbage down to the street, and she carried up water, stopping at each floor to catch her breath. And, dressed in cheap housedresses, she went to the fruit dealer, the grocer, the butchers, with her basket under her arms, haggling, insulting, defending her measly cash penny by penny.

100 They had to make installment payments every month, and, to buy more time, to refinance loans.

The husband worked evenings to make fair copies of tradesmen's accounts, and late into the night he made copies at five cents a page.

And this life lasted ten years.

At the end of ten years, they had paid back everything—everything—including the extra charges imposed by loan sharks and the accumulation of compound interest.

Mrs. Loisel looked old now. She had become the strong, hard, and rude woman of poor households. Her hair unkempt, with uneven skirts and rough, red hands, she spoke loudly, washed floors with large buckets of water. But sometimes, when her husband was at work, she sat down near the window, and she dreamed of that evening so long ago, of that party, where she had been so beautiful and so admired.

105 What would life have been like if she had not lost that necklace? Who knows? Who knows? Life is so peculiar, so uncertain. How little a thing it takes to destroy you or to save you!

Well, one Sunday, when she had gone for a stroll along the Champs-Elysées to relax from the cares of the week, she suddenly noticed a woman walking with a child. It was Mrs. Forrestier, still youthful, still beautiful, still attractive.

Mrs. Loisel felt moved. Would she speak to her? Yes, certainly. And now that she had paid, she could tell all. Why not?

She walked closer.

"Hello, Jeanne."

110 The other gave no sign of recognition and was astonished to be addressed so familiarly by this working-class woman. She stammered:

"But . . . Madam! . . . I don't know. . . . You must have made a mistake."

"No. I'm Mathilde Loisel."

Her friend cried out:

"Oh! . . . My poor Mathilde, you've changed so much."

115 "Yes. I've had some tough times since I saw you last; in fact hardships . . . and all because of you! . . ."

"Of me . . . how so?"

"You remember the diamond necklace that you lent me to go to the party at the Ministry of Education?"

"Yes. What then?"

"Well, I lost it."

120 "How, since you gave it back to me?"

"I returned another exactly like it. And for ten years we've been paying for it. You understand this wasn't easy for us, who have nothing. . . . Finally it's over, and I'm damned glad."

Mrs. Forrestier stopped her.

"You say that you bought a diamond necklace to replace mine?"

"Yes, you didn't notice it, eh? It was exactly like yours."

125   And she smiled with proud and childish joy.

Mrs. Forrestier, deeply moved, took both her hands.

"Oh, my poor Mathilde! But mine was only costume jewelry. At most, it was worth only five hundred francs! ..."

Reading and Responding in a Computer File or Notebook

As you read the various works assigned in your courses, you should develop the indispensable habit of active reading and responding. In practice, you may use the margins in your text to record comments and questions, but you should also plan to record your more lengthy responses in a notebook, on note cards, on separate sheets of paper, or in a computer file. Be careful not to lose anything. Keep *all* your notes. As you progress from reading one work to the next, you will find that your written or saved comments will be immensely important as your journal of first impressions, together with your more carefully considered and expanded thoughts.

In keeping your notebook, your objective should be to learn assigned works inside and out and then write perceptive comments about them. To achieve this goal, you will need to read the work more than once. Develop a good note-taking system so that as you read, you will create a "memory bank" of your own knowledge. You can make withdrawals from this fund of ideas when you begin to write.

Guidelines for Reading: Preparation for Writing

1. Observations for basic understanding

    a. Explain words, situations, and concepts. Write down words that are new or not immediately clear. Make liberal use of your dictionary, and record the relevant meanings in your notebook. Write down special difficulties so that you can ask your instructor about them.

b. Determine what is happening in the work. For a story or play, where do the actions take place? What do they show? Who is involved? Who is the major figure? Why is he or she major? What relationships do the characters have with one another? What concerns do the characters have? What do they do? Who says what to whom? How do the speeches advance the action and reveal the characters? For a poem, what is the situation? Who is talking, and to whom? What does the speaker say about the situation? Why does the poem end how and where it does?

2. Notes on first impressions

a. Make a record of your reactions and responses. What did you think was memorable, noteworthy, funny, or otherwise striking? Did you worry, get scared, laugh, smile, feel a thrill, learn a great deal, feel proud, find a lot to think about?

b. Describe interesting characterizations, events, techniques, and ideas. If you like a character or an idea, explain what you like about it, and do the same for characters and ideas you don't like. Is there anything else in the work that you especially like or dislike? Are certain parts easy or difficult to understand? Why? Are there any surprises? What was your reaction to them? Be sure to use your own words when writing your explanations.

3. Development of ideas and enlargement of responses

a. Trace developing patterns. Make an outline or a scheme: What conflicts appear? Do these conflicts exist between people, groups, or ideas? How are the conflicts resolved? Is one force, idea, or side the winner? How do you respond to the winner or to the loser?

b. Write expanded notes about characters, situations, and actions. What explanations need to be made about the characters? What is the nature of the situations (e.g., young people discover a damaged boat, and themselves, in the spring; a prisoner tries to hide her baby from cruel guards; and so on)? What is the nature of the actions (e.g., a mother and daughter go shopping; a series of strangers intrude upon a christening celebration; a woman is told that her husband has been killed in a train wreck; a group of children are taken to a fashionable toy store; and so on)? What are the people like, and what are their habits and customs? What sort of language do they use?

c. Memorize important, interesting, and well-written passages. Copy them in full on note cards, and keep these in your pocket or purse. When walking to class, riding public transportation, or otherwise not occupying your time, learn them by heart. Please take memorization seriously.

d. Always write down questions that come up during your reading. You may raise these in class, and trying to write your own answers will aid your study.

Sample Notebook or Journal Entries on Maupassant's "The Necklace"

The following entries demonstrate how you can use the foregoing guidelines in your first thoughts about a work. You should try to develop enough observations and responses to be useful later, both for additional study and for developing essays. Notice that the entries are not only comments, but also questions.

> Early in the story, Mathilde seems to be spoiled. She and her husband are not well off, but she is unable to face her own situation.
>
> She is a dreamer but seems harmless. Her daydreams about a fancy home, with all the expensive belongings, are not unusual. It would be unusual to find people who do not have such dreams.
>
> She is embarrassed by her husband's taste for plain food. The storyteller contrasts her taste for trout and quail with Loisel's cheaper favorites.
>
> When the Loisels get the invitation to the ball, Mathilde becomes difficult. Her wish for an expensive dress (the cost of Loisel's shotgun) creates a problem, and she creates another problem by wanting to wear fine jewelry.
>
> Her change in character can be related to the places in the story: the Street of Martyrs, the dinner party scene, the attic

flat. Also, she fills the places she daydreams about with the most expensive things she can imagine.

Her success at the party shows that she has the charm the storyteller talks about in paragraph 2. She seems never to have had any other chance to exert her power.

The worst part of her personality is shown in rushing away from the party because she is ashamed of her ordinary and shabby shawl, which she had worn because the party takes place in January. It is Mathilde's unhappiness and unwillingness to adjust to her modest means that cause the financial downfall of the Loisels. This disaster is her fault.

Borrowing the money to replace the necklace shows that both Loisel and Mathilde have a strong sense of honor. Making up the loss is good, even if it destroys them financially.

There are some nice touches, like Loisel's seeming to be five years older (11) and his staying with the other husbands of women enjoying themselves (9). These are well done.

It's too bad that Loisel and Mathilde don't confess to Jeanne that the jewels are lost. Their pride or their honor stops them—or perhaps their fear of being accused of theft.

Their ten years of slavish work (12) show how they have come down in life. Mathilde does all her work by hand, so she really does pitch in and is, as the narrator says, heroic.

The attic flat is important. Mathilde becomes loud and frumpy when living there (12-13), but she also develops strength. She does what she has to. The earlier apartment and the elegance of her imaginary rooms had brought out her limitations.

The setting of the Champs-Elysees also reflects her character, for she feels free there to tell Jeanne about the disastrous loss and the ten years of sacrifice (13), producing the surprise ending. A curious point: Is it likely that Mathilde would not have had contact with Mrs. Forrestier during that ten-year period?

The narrator's statement, "How little a thing it takes to destroy you or to save you!" (13) is full of thought. The necklace is little, and it makes a gigantic problem. This creates the story's irony.

QUESTIONS: Is this story more about the surprise ending or about the character of Mathilde? Is she to be condemned or admired? Does the outcome stem from the little things that make us or break us, as the narrator suggests, or from the difficulty of rising above one's economic class, which seems true, or both? What do the speaker's remarks about women's status mean? This probably isn't relevant, but wouldn't Jeanne, after hearing about the substitution, give the full value of the necklace to the Loisels (or at least return the necklace to them), and wouldn't they then be pretty well off?

⟋

These are reasonable—and also fairly full—remarks and observations about "The Necklace." Use your notebook or journal similarly for all reading assignments. If your assignment is simply to learn about a work, general notes like these should be enough. If you are preparing for a test, you might write pointed observations more in line with what is happening in your class, and also write and answer your own questions. If you have a writing assignment, observations like these can help you focus more closely on your topic—such as character, idea, or setting. Whatever your purpose, always take good notes, and put in as many details and responses as you can. The notes will be invaluable to you as a refresher, and as a wellspring of thought.

3

DISCOVERING IDEAS

Finished writing is the sharpened, focused expression of thought and study. It begins with the search for something to say—an idea. Not all ideas are equal; some are better than others, and getting good ideas is a skill that will develop the more you reflect and write. As you discover ideas and explain them in words, you will also improve your perceptions and increase your critical faculties.

In addition, because literature itself contains the subject material (though not in a systematic way) of philosophy, religion, psychology, sociology, and politics, learning to analyze literature and to write about it will also improve your capacity to deal with these and other disciplines.

The Goal of Writing: To Show a Process of Thought

As you approach the task of writing, keep in mind that your goal should always be to *explain* the work you are analyzing. You should never be satisfied with simply restating the events in the work. Too often, students fall into a pattern of retelling a story or play, or summarizing the details of a poem. But nothing could be farther from what is expected in good writing. **Good writing should be the embodiment of your thought; it should show your thought in action.** Thinking is an active process that does not happen accidentally. Thinking requires that you develop ideas, draw conclusions, exemplify them and support them with details, and then connect everything in a coherent manner. Your goal should constantly be to explain the results of your thinking—your ideas, your play of mind over the materials of a work, your insights, your conclusions.

Approach each writing assignment in light of the following objectives: You should consider your reader as a person who has read the work, just as you have done. This person knows what is in the work, and therefore does not need you to restate what she or he already knows. Instead, your reader wants to learn from you what to think about it. Therefore, always, your task as a writer is to explain something about the work, to describe the thoughts that you can develop about it. Let us consider again Maupassant's "The Necklace." We have recognized that the main character, Mathilde Loisel, is a young Parisian housewife who is married to a minor clerk in the Ministry of Education. We know this, but if we are reading an essay about the story we will want to learn more. Let us then suppose that a first goal of one of your paragraphs is to explain the deep dissatisfaction Mathilde feels in the early part of the story. Your paragraph might go as follows:

> In the early part of the story, Maupassant establishes that Mathilde is deeply dissatisfied with her life. Her threadbare furniture and drab walls are a cause of her unhappiness. Under these circumstances her daydreams of beautiful rooms staffed by "elegant valets," together with a number of rooms for intimate conversations with friends, multiply her dissatisfaction. The meager meals that she shares with her husband make her imagine sumptuous banquets that she feels are rightfully hers by birth but that are denied her because of her circumstances. The emphasis in these early scenes of the story is always on Mathilde's discontentment and frustration.

Notice that this paragraph does not simply restate the story's events, but rather refers to the events in order to explain to us, as readers, the causes for Mathilde's unhappiness. The paragraph illustrates your process of thought. Here is another way in which you might use a thought to connect the same materials:

In the early part of the story, Maupassant emphasizes
the economic difficulty of Mathilde's life. The threadbare furniture and ugly curtains, for example, highlight
that there is no money to purchase better things. The
same sparseness of existence is shown by the meager
meals that she shares with her husband. With the
capacity to appreciate better things, Mathilde is forced
by circumstances to make do with worse. Her dreams of
sumptuous banquets are therefore natural, given her
level of frustration with the life around her. In short,
her unhappiness is an understandable consequence of her
aversion to her plain and drab apartment and the
tightness of money.

Here, the details are substantially the same as in the first paragraph, but they are unified by a different idea—namely the economic constraints of Mathilde's life. What is important is that neither paragraph retells only the details. Instead, the paragraphs illustrate the goal of writing with a purpose. *Whenever you write, you should always be trying, as in these examples, to use a governing thought or thoughts to shape the details in the work you are analyzing.*

For both practiced and beginning writers alike, there are four stages of thinking and writing, and in each of these there are characteristic activities. (1) In the beginning stage, writers try to find the details and thoughts that seem to be right for eventual inclusion in what they are hoping to write. (2) The next (or middle) stage is characterized by written drafts, or sketches—ideas, sentences, paragraphs. (3) An advanced stage of writing is the forming and ordering of what has previously been done—the creation and determination of a final essay. Although these stages occur in a natural order, they are not separate and distinct, but merge with each other and in effect are fused together. However, when you think you are close to finishing your essay, you may find that you are not as close as you thought. (4) You are now in the finishing or completing stage, when you need to include something else, something more, something different, and something to make things complete. At this point, you can easily revisit an earlier stage to discover new details and ideas. You might say that your work is always tentative until you regard it as finished, or until you need to turn it in.

Discovering Ideas ("Brainstorming")

With the foregoing general goal in mind, let us assume that you have read the assigned work and have made your own notes and observations. You are now ready to consider and plan what to include in your essay. This earliest stage of writing is unpredictable and somewhat frustrating because you are on a search. You do not know quite what you want—you are reaching out for ideas—not yet sure what they are and what you might say about them. This process of searching and discovery, sometimes also called *brainstorming*, requires you to examine any and every subject that your mind can produce.

Just as you are trying to reach for ideas, however, you should also try to introduce purpose and resolution into your thinking. You have to zero in on something specific, and develop your ideas through this process. Although what you first write may seem indefinite, the best approach is to put your mind, figuratively, into specific channels or grooves, and then confine your thoughts within these boundaries. What matters is to focus on a particular topic and get your thoughts down on paper or onto a computer screen. Once you can see your thoughts in front of you, you can work with them and develop them.

You can consider literary works in many ways, but for now, as a way of getting started, you might choose to explore the work's (1) characters, (2) historical period and background, (3) social and economic conditions, (4) major ideas, (5) artistic qualities, or (6) any additional ideas that seem important to you. These topics, of course, have many subtopics, but any one of them can help you in the concentration you will need for beginning your essay (and also for classroom discussion). All you need is one topic, just one; don't try everything at the same time.

Study the Characters in the Work

You do not need to be a professional psychologist to discuss the persons or characters you find in a work. You only need to raise issues about the characters and what they do and what they represent. What are the characters like at the beginning of the work?

What happens to them? Do they do anything that causes them to change, and how are they changed? Are the changes for good or for bad? Why do the characters do the things they do? What do they do correctly? What do they do incorrectly? Why? For example, in "The Necklace," Mathilde is wrong not to tell Jeanne about the lost necklace. Such an immediate admission of truth would have saved her and her husband ten years of hardship and deprivation. But Mathilde does not tell the truth. Why not? What do we learn about her character because she avoids or ignores this admission?

In discussing character, you might also wish to raise the issue of whether the characters in the work do, or do not do, what might normally be expected from people in their circumstances. Do they correspond to type? The idea here is that certain attitudes and behaviors are typical of people at particular stages of life (e.g., children behaving like children, lovers dealing with their relationship, a young couple coping with difficult finances). Thus, we might ask questions about whether the usual circumstances experienced by the characters affect them, either by limiting them in some way or by freeing them. What attitudes seem typical of the characters? How do these attitudes govern what the characters do, or do not do? For example, one of the most typical circumstances of life is marriage. According to the positive and ideal type of marriage, partners should be forthcoming with each other; they should tell each other things and should not conceal what is on their minds. If they have problems, they should discuss them and try to solve them together. In "The Necklace" we see that Mathilde and Loisel do not show these desired qualities, and their absence of communication can be seen as an element in their financial catastrophe. However, during their long years of trouble they work together; they eventually exhibit the quality of honesty, and in this respect they fulfill their role, or type, as a married couple.

An analysis of typical attitudes themselves can also furnish you with material for discussion. For example, Mathilde, who is a member of the lower commercial class, has attitudes that are more appropriate to the upper or leisure class. She does not have the resources to bridge this gap, however, and her frustration causes her to nag her husband to give her enough money to live out her dream, if only for a moment.

Determine the Work's Historical Period and Background

An obvious topic is the historical circumstances of the work. When was the work written? How well does it portray details about life at the time it appeared? What is historically unique about it? To what degree does it help you learn something about the past that you did not previously know? What actions in the work are like or unlike actions going on at the present time? What truthfulness to life do you discover in the work? In "The Necklace," for example, which was published more than a century ago, Mathilde's duty is to stay at home as a housewife—a traditional role—while her husband is the family breadwinner. After the loss of the necklace she can no longer afford domestic help, and she is compelled to do all her own housework and her own shopping. She has none of today's home conveniences—no dishwasher, microwave, refrigerator, or car. Her husband, a clerk or secretary-copyist, spends his workday copying business records by hand, for at the period of the story there were few typewriters and absolutely no computers. Discussing matters like these might also help you with works written during modern times, because our own assumptions, artifacts, and habits are open to analysis and discussion.

Analyze the Work's Economic and Social Conditions

Closely related to the historical period, another obvious topic to pursue in many works is the economic and social condition of the characters. What are the characters' economic and social levels? How are events in the work related to their condition? How does their money, or lack of it, limit what they do? How do their economic circumstances either restrict or liberate their imaginations? How do their jobs and their apparent income determine their way of life? If we ask some of these questions about "The Necklace," as we have seen, we find that Mathilde and her husband are greatly burdened by their lack of money, and also that their obligation to repay their huge loan drives them into economic want and sacrifice.

An important part of the economic and social analysis of literature is the consideration of female characters and what it means to
be a woman. This is the *feminist analysis* of literature, which asks
questions like these: What role is Mathilde compelled to take as a
result of her gender and family background? How does Jeanne Forrestier's way of life contrast with that of Mathilde? What can
Mathilde do with her life? To what degree is she limited by her role
as a housewife? Does she have any chance of an occupation outside
the home? How does her economic condition cause her to yearn for
better things? What causes her to borrow the necklace? What is her
contribution, as a woman, to the repayment of the loans? Should
Mathilde's limited life in "The Necklace" be considered as a political argument for greater freedom for women? Once you start asking questions like these, you will find that your thinking is
developing along with your ideas for writing.

The feminist approach to the interpretation of literature has
been well established, and it will usually provide you with a way to
discuss a work. It is also possible, of course, to analyze what a
work says about the condition of being a man, or being a child.
Depending on the work, many of the questions important in a feminist approach are not dissimilar to those you might use when dealing with childhood or male adulthood.

One of the most important social and economic topics is that of
race and ethnicity. What happens in the work that seems to occur
mainly because of the race of the characters? Is the author pointing
out any deprivations, any absence of opportunity, any oppression?
What do the characters do under such circumstances? Do they suc-
ceed or not? Are they negative? Are they angry? Are they resolute
and determined? Your aim in an inquiry of this type should be to
concentrate on actions and ideas in the work that are clearly
related to race.

Explain the Work's Major Ideas

One effective way of focusing on a work is to zero in on ideas, val-
ues, or issues to be discovered there. What ideas might we gain
from the story of the lengthy but needless sacrifice and drudgery
experienced by Mathilde and her husband? The speaker presents

one obvious and acceptable idea: that even the smallest, most accidental incident can cause immense consequences. This is an idea that we might expand and illustrate in an entire essay. Here are some other ideas that we might also pursue, all of them based on the story's actions:

- Many actions have unforeseeable and uncontrollable consequences.
- Lack of communication is a significant cause of hardship.
- Adversity might bring out a character's good—or bad—qualities.
- Mutual effort enables people to overcome difficulties.

These themes are all to be found in Maupassant's story. In other works, of course, we might find comparable themes, in addition to other major ideas and issues.

Describe the Work's Artistic Qualities

A work's artistic qualities provide many possible topics for studying, but for our purposes, you may consider matters such as the work's plan or organization and the author's narrative method, writing style, or poetic techniques. Thus, in "The Necklace," we observe that almost the entire story develops with Mathilde at the center. At first, the story brings us close to her, for we are told of her dissatisfaction and impatience with her surroundings. As the story progresses, the storyteller/speaker presents Mathilde's person and actions more objectively, and also more distantly.

Another artistic approach would be to determine the story's pattern of development—how, chronologically, the loss of the necklace brings financial misfortune to the Loisels. We might also look for the author's inclusion of symbols in the story, such as the name of the street where the Loisels originally live, their move to an attic flat, or the roughness of Mathilde's hands as a result of her constant housework. There are many other ways to consider the formal aspects of a literary work.

Explain Any Other Approaches That Seem Important

Additional ways of looking at a work such as "The Necklace" might occur to you, beyond those just described. One reader might raise the issue that the story's speaker seems to exhibit a particularly patronizing attitude toward women. He draws attention to Mathilde's joy because of the party, and generalizes about how her "victory" was so "sweet to the heart of any woman" (9). As a writer analyzing "The Necklace," you might raise the issue of Maupassant's attitude toward women in light of this sentence. Another aspect of the story might be the way in which Mathilde's physical appearance undergoes change as a result of her dismissing the maid and taking on the household chores herself. Still another aspect is the attitude of Loisel and his relationship with Mathilde, for he seems rather distant from Mathilde's concerns. The story tells nothing about his reactions to the misfortune beyond how he pitches in to restore the borrowed money, almost to the point of enslaving himself to the task. Would he never have uttered any reproachful words toward his wife? The point here is that additional ideas may suggest themselves to you, and that you should keep yourself open to explore and discuss any of these other ways of seeing and thinking.

4

PREPARING TO WRITE

By this time, you will have been focusing on your topic and will have assembled much that you can put into your essay. You should now aim to develop paragraphs and sketches of what you will eventually include. You should think constantly of the point or argument you want to develop, but invariably digressions will occur, together with other difficulties—false starts, dead ends, total cessation of thought, digressions, and general frustration.

Remember, however, that it is important just to start. Jump right in and start writing anything at all—no matter how unacceptable your first efforts may seem—and force yourself to deal with the materials. The writing down of ideas does not commit you. You should not think that these first ideas are untouchable and holy just because you have written them on paper or see them on your computer screen. You can throw them out in favor of new ideas, you can make cross-outs and changes, and you can move paragraphs or even sections around as you wish. However, if you do not start writing, your first thoughts will remain locked in your mind and you will have nothing to work with. You must learn to accept the uncertainties in the writing process and make them work *for* you rather than *against* you.

Build Ideas from Your Original Notes

You need to get your mind going by mining your notebook or computer files for useful things you have already written. Thus, let us use an observation in our original set of notes—"The attic flat is important"—in reference to the poorer rooms where Mathilde and her husband live while they are repaying their creditors. With such a note as a start, you might develop a number of ideas to support an argument about Mathilde's character, as in the following:

> The attic flat is important. Early in the story, in her apartment, Mathilde is dreamy and impractical. She seems delicate, but after losing the necklace, she is delicate no longer. She becomes a worker after they move to the flat. She does a lot more when living there.
>
> In the flat, Mathilde has to sacrifice. She gives up her servant, washes greasy pots, climbs stairs carrying buckets of water, sloshes water around to clean floors, and does all the clothes washing by hand.
>
> When living in the flat she gets stronger, but she also becomes loud and common. She argues with shopkeepers to get the lowest prices. She stops caring for herself. There is a reversal here, from incapable and well groomed to capable but coarse.

In this way, even in an assertion as basic as "The attic flat is important," the process of putting together details is a form of concentrated thought that leads you creatively forward. You can now express thoughts and conclusions that you could not express at the beginning. Such an exercise in stretching your mind leads you to put elements of the work together in ways that create ideas for good essays.

Trace Patterns of Action and Thought

You can also discover ideas by making a list or scheme for the story or main idea. What conflicts appear? Do these conflicts exist between people, groups, or ideas? How does the author resolve them? Is one force, idea, or side the winner? Why? How do you respond to the winner or to the loser? Using this method, you might make a list similar to this one:

> At the beginning, Mathilde is a fish out of water. She dreams of wealth, but her life is drab and her husband is dull.
>
> When the Loisels get the dinner invitation Mathilde pouts and whines. Her husband feels discomfort when she manipulates him into buying her an expensive party dress.
>
> Her world of daydreams hurts her real life when her desire for wealth causes her to borrow the necklace. Losing the necklace is just plain bad luck.

These arguments all focus on Mathilde's character, but you may wish to trace other patterns you find in the story. If you start planning an essay about another pattern, be sure to account for all the actions and scenes that relate to your topic. Otherwise, you might miss a piece of evidence that could lead you to new conclusions.

Raise and Answer Your Own Questions

A good habit you should cultivate is to raise your own questions, and try to answer them as you consider your reading. The guidelines for reading will help you formulate questions (pp. 14–16), but you can raise additional questions like these:

- What is happening as the work unfolds? How does an action at the beginning of the work bring about later actions and speeches?
- Who are the main characters? What seems unusual or different about what they do in the work?
- What conclusions can you draw about the work's actions, scenes, and situations? Explain these conclusions.
- What are the characters and speakers like? What do they do and say about themselves, their goals, the people around them, their families, their friends, their work, and the general circumstances of their lives?
- What kinds of words do the characters use: formal or informal words, slang or profanity?
- What literary conventions and devices have you discovered, and how do these affect the work? (When an author addresses readers directly, for example, that is a convention; when a

comparison is used, that is a device, which might be either a metaphor or a simile.)

Of course, you can raise other questions as you reread the piece, or you can be left with one or two major questions that you decide to pursue.

Put Ideas Together Using a Plus-Minus, Pro-Con, or Either-Or Method

A common and very helpful method of discovering ideas is to develop a set of contrasts: plus-minus, pro-con, either-or. Let us suppose a plus-minus method of considering the following question about Mathilde: Should she be "admired" (plus) or "condemned" (minus)?

Plus: Admired?	Minus: Condemned?
After she cries when they get the invitation, she recovers with a "strong effort"-maybe she doesn't want her husband to feel bad.	She wants to be envied and admired only for being attractive and intriguing, not for more important qualities. She seems spoiled and selfish.
She scores a great victory at the dance. She really does have the power to charm and captivate.	She wastes her time in daydreaming about things she can't have, and she whines because she is unhappy.
Once she loses the necklace, she and her husband become poor and deprived. But she does "her share . . . completely, heroically" (12) to make up for the loss.	Even though the Loisels live poorly, Mathilde manipulates her husband into giving her more money than they can afford for a party dress.
Even when she is poor, she dreams about that marvelous, shining moment at the great ball. This is pathetic, because Mathilde gets worse than she deserves.	She assumes that her friend Jeanne would think her a thief if she admitted losing the necklace. Shouldn't she have had more confidence in Jeanne?

Plus: Admired?	Minus: Condemned?
At the end, after everything is paid back, and her reputation is secure, Mathilde confesses the loss to Jeanne.	She becomes loud and coarse and haggles about pennies, thus undergoing a cheapening of her person and manner.

By putting contrasting observations side by side in this way, you will find that ideas start to come naturally, which will be helpful to you when you begin writing, regardless of how you finally organize your essay. It is possible, for example, that you might develop either column as the argumentative basis of an essay, or you might use your notes to support the idea that Mathilde is too complex to be either wholly admired or wholly condemned. You might also want to introduce an entirely new topic of development, such as that Mathilde should be pitied rather than condemned or admired. In short, arranging materials in the plus-minus pattern is a powerful way to discover ideas—a truly helpful habit of promoting thought—that can lead to ways of development that you do not at first realize.

Originate and Develop Your Thoughts Through Writing

You should always write down what you are thinking, for, as a principle, *unwritten thought is incomplete thought*. Make a practice of writing your observations about the work, in addition to any questions that occur to you. This is an exciting step in preliminary writing because it can be useful when you write later drafts. You will discover that reviewing what you have written not only enables you to correct and improve the writing you have done, but it can also lead you to recognize that you need more. The process goes just about like this: "Something needs to be added here—important details that my reader will not have noticed, new support for my argument, a new idea that has just occurred to me, a significant connection to link my thoughts." If you follow such a process, you will be using your own written ideas to create new ideas. You will be advancing your own abilities as a thinker and writer.

The processes just described of searching for ideas, or brainstorming, are useful for you at any stage of composition. Even when you are fairly close to finishing your essay, you might suddenly recognize that you need to add something more (or subtract something you don't like). When that happens, you may return to the discovery or brainstorming process to initiate and develop new ideas and new arguments.

5

MAKE AN INITIAL DRAFT
OF YOUR ESSAY

As you use the brainstorming and focusing techniques, you are also, in fact, beginning your essay. You will need to revise your ideas as connections among them become clearer and as you reexamine the work to discover details to support the argument you are making. By this stage, however, you already have many of the raw materials you need for developing your topic.

Base Your Essay on a Central Idea, Argument, or Statement

By definition, an *essay* is an organized, connected, and fully developed set of paragraphs that expand on a central idea, central argument, or central statement. All parts of an essay should contribute to the reader's understanding of the idea. To achieve unity and completeness, each paragraph refers to the *central argument* and demonstrates how selected details from the work relate to it and support it. The *central idea* helps you control and shape your essay, just as it also provides guidance for your reader.

A successful essay about literature is a brief but thorough (not exhaustive) examination of a literary work in light of topics like those we have already raised—character, background, economic conditions, circumstances of gender, major ideas, artistic qualities, and any additional topic, such as point of view and symbolism.

Central ideas or arguments might be (1) that a character is strong and tenacious, or (2) that the story shows the unpredictability of action, or (3) that the point of view makes the action seem "distant and objective," or (4) that a major symbol governs the actions and thoughts of the main characters. In essays on these topics, all materials must be tied to such central ideas or arguments. Thus, it is a fact that in "The Necklace," Mathilde endures ten years of slavish work and sacrifice as she and her husband accumulate enough money to repay their monumental debt. This we know, but it is not relevant to an essay on her character unless you connect it by a central argument showing how it demonstrates one of her major traits—her growing strength and perseverance.

Look through all of your ideas for one or two that catch your eye for development. In all the early stages of preliminary writing, the chances are that you have already discovered at least a few ideas that are more thought provoking, or more important, than the others.

Once you choose an idea you think you can work with, write it as a complete sentence that is essential to the argument of your essay. A simple phrase such as "setting and character" does not focus thought the way a sentence does. The following sentence moves the topic toward new exploration and discovery because it combines a topic with an outcome: *The setting of "The Necklace" reflects Mathilde's character.* You can choose to be even more specific: *Mathilde's strengths and weaknesses are reflected in the real and imaginary places in "The Necklace."*

Now that you have phrased a single, central idea or argument for your essay, you have also established a guide by which you can accept, reject, rearrange, and change the ideas you have been planning to develop. You can now draft a few paragraphs to see whether your idea seems valid (you may base the paragraphs on some of the sketches you have already made; always use as many of your early observations as possible), or you might decide that it would be more helpful to make an outline or a list before you do more writing. In either case, you should use your notes for evidence to connect to your central idea. If you need to bolster your argument with more supporting details and ideas, go once again to the techniques of discovery and brainstorming.

Using the central idea that the changes in the story's settings reflect Mathilde's character might produce a paragraph like the following, which presents an argument about her negative qualities:

```
     The original apartment in the Street of Martyrs and
the dream world of wealthy places both show negative
sides of Mathilde's character. The real-life apartment,
though livable, is shabby. The furnishings all bring out
her discontent. The shabbiness makes her think only of
luxuriousness, and having one servant girl causes her to
dream of having many servants. The luxury of her dream
life heightens her unhappiness with what she actually has.
```

In such a preliminary draft, in which the purpose is to connect details and thoughts to the major idea, many details from the story are used in support. In the final draft, this kind of support is essential.

Create a Thesis Sentence as Your Guide to Organization

With your central idea or argument as your focus, you can decide which of the earlier observations and ideas can be developed further. Your goal is to establish a number of major topics to support your argument and to express them in a *thesis sentence* or *thesis statement*—an organizing sentence that contains the major topics you plan to treat in your essay. Suppose you choose three ideas from your discovery stage of development. If you put the central idea at the left and the list of topics at the right, you have the shape of the thesis sentence. Note that the first two topics below are taken from the discovery paragraph.

Central Idea	Topics
The setting of "The Necklace" reflects Mathilde's character.	1. First apartment 2. Dream-life mansion rooms 3. Attic flat

This arrangement leads to the following thesis statement or thesis sentence:

```
Mathilde's character growth is connected to her first
apartment, her dream-life mansion rooms, and her attic
flat.
```

You can revise the thesis sentence at any stage of the writing process if you find that you do not have enough evidence from the work to support it. Perhaps a new topic will occur to you, and you can include it, appropriately, as a part of your thesis sentence.

As we have seen, the central idea or central argument is the "glue" of the essay. The thesis sentence lists the parts to be fastened together—that is, the topics in which the central idea is to be demonstrated and argued. To alert your readers to your essay's structure, the thesis sentence is usually placed at the end of the introductory paragraph, just before the body of the essay.

As you write your first draft, you need to support the points of your thesis sentence with your notes and discovery materials. You can alter, reject, and rearrange ideas and details as you wish, as long as you change your thesis sentence to account for the changes. (For this reason, many writers write their introductions last.) The thesis sentence just shown contains three topics (it could be two, or four, or more) to be used in forming the body of the essay.

The Need for a Sound Argument in Writing about Literature

As you write about literature, you should always try to connect your explanations to a specific argument; that is, you are writing about a specific work, but you are trying to prove—or argue—or demonstrate—a point or idea about it. This book provides you with a number of separate subjects relating to the study of literature. As you select one of these and begin writing, however, you are not to explain just that such-and-such a story has a character that changes and grows, or that such-and-such a poem contains the thought that nature creates great beauty. Rather, you should assert the importance of your topic to the work as a whole in relation to a specific point or argument. One example of an argument might be that a story's first-person point of view permits readers to draw their own conclusions about the speaker's character. Another argument might be that the poet's thought is shown in a poem's details about the bustling sounds and sights of animals in springtime.

Let us therefore repeat and stress that your writing *should always have an argumentative edge*—a goal of demonstrating the truth of your conclusions and clarifying and illuminating your idea about the topic and also about the work. It is here that the accuracy of your choices of details from the work, the soundness of your conclusions, and the cumulative weight of your evidence are essential. You cannot allow your main ideas to rest on one detail alone, but must support your conclusions by showing that the bulk of material leads to them and that they are linked in a reasonable chain of fact and logic. Such clarification is the goal of argumentation.

Begin Each Paragraph with a Topic Sentence

Just as the organization of the entire essay is based on the thesis, the form of each paragraph is based on its *topic sentence*—an assertion about how a topic from the predicate of the thesis statement supports the argument contained or implied in the central idea. The first topic in our example is the relationship of Mathilde's character to her first apartment, and the resulting paragraph should emphasize this relationship. If your topic is the coarsening of her character during the ten-year travail, you can then form a topic sentence by connecting the trait with the location, as follows:

```
The attic flat reflects the coarsening of Mathilde's
character.
```

Beginning with this sentence, the paragraph will present details that argue how Mathilde's rough, heavy housework changes her behavior, appearance, and general outlook.

Use Your Topic Sentences as the Arguments for Your Paragraph Development

Once you create a topic sentence, you can use it to focus your observations and conclusions. Let us see how our topic about the attic flat can be developed in a paragraph of argument:

<u>The attic flat reflects the coarsening of Mathilde's</u>
<u>character</u>. Maupassant emphasizes the burdens Mathilde

```
endures to save money, such as mopping floors, cleaning
greasy and encrusted pots and pans, taking out the
garbage, and washing clothes and dishes by hand. This
work makes her rough and coarse, an effect also shown by
her giving up care of her hair and hands, wearing the
cheapest dresses possible, haggling with the local
shopkeepers, and becoming loud and penny-pinching. If at
the beginning she is delicate and attractive, at the end
she is unpleasant and coarse.
```

Here, details from the story are introduced to provide support for the topic sentence. All the subjects—the hard work, the lack of personal care, the wearing of cheap dresses, and the haggling with the shopkeepers—are introduced not to retell the story but rather to exemplify the argument the writer is making about Mathilde's character.

Referring to the Names of Authors

As a general principle, for both men and women writers, you should regularly include the author's *full name* in the *first sentence* of your essay. Here are model first sentences:

```
Shirley Jackson's "The Lottery" is a story featuring
both suspense and horror.

"The Lottery," by Shirley Jackson, is a story fea-
turing both suspense and horror.
```

For all later references, use only last names, such as *Jackson, Maupassant, Lawrence,* or *Porter.* However, for the "giants" of literature, you should use the last names exclusively. In referring to writers like Shakespeare and Dickinson, for example, there is no need to include *William* or *Emily.*

In spite of today's informal standards, never use an author's first name alone, as in "*Shirley* skillfully creates suspense and horror in 'The Lottery.'" Also, do not use a courtesy title before the names of dead authors, such as "*Ms.* Jackson's 'The Lottery' is a suspenseful horror story," or "*Mr.* Shakespeare's idea is that information is uncertain." Use the last names alone.

As with all conventions, of course, there are exceptions. If you are referring to a childhood work of a writer, the first name might be appropriate, but be sure to shift to the last name when referring to the writer's mature works. If your writer has a professional or a noble title, such as "*Lord* Byron" or "*Queen* Elizabeth I," it is not improper to use the title. Even then, however, the titles are commonly omitted for males, so that most references to Lord Byron and Alfred, Lord Tennyson, should be simply to "Byron" and "Tennyson."

Referring to living authors is somewhat problematical. Some journals and newspapers often use the courtesy titles *Mr.* and *Ms.* in their reviews. However, scholarly journals, which are likely to remain on library shelves and Web sites for many decades, follow the general principle of beginning with the entire name and then using only the last name for later references.

Select Only One Topic—No More— for Each Paragraph

You should treat each separate topic in a single paragraph—one topic, one paragraph. However, if a topic seems especially difficult, long, and heavily detailed, you can divide it into two or more subtopics, each receiving a separate paragraph of its own—two or more subtopics, two or more separate paragraphs. Should you make this division, your topic then is really a section, and each paragraph in the section should have its own topic sentence.

Develop an Outline as the Means of Organizing Your Essay

So far, we have been creating a de facto *outline*—that is, a skeletal plan of organization. Some writers never use any outline but prefer informal lists of ideas; others always rely on outlines; still others insist that they cannot make an outline until they have finished writing. And then there are those writers who simply hate outlines.

Regardless of your preference, your final essay should have a tight structure. Therefore, you should use a guiding outline to develop and shape your essay.

The outline we focus on here is the *analytical sentence outline*. This type is easier to create than it sounds. It consists of (1) an introduction, including the central idea and the thesis sentence, together with (2) topic sentences that are to be used in each paragraph of the body, followed by (3) a conclusion. When applied to the subject we have been developing, such an outline looks like this:

```
        Title: How Setting in "The Necklace"
        Is Connected to Mathilde's Character

1. Introduction
    a. Central idea: Maupassant uses setting to show
       Mathilde's character.
    b. Thesis statement: Her first apartment brings
       out her character growth, her daydreams about
       elegant rooms in a mansion, and her attic flat.

2. Body: Topic sentences a, b, and c (and d, e, and f,
   if necessary)
    a. Details about her first apartment explain her
       dissatisfaction and depression.
    b. Her daydreams about mansion rooms are like the
       apartment because they too make her unhappy.
    c. The attic flat reflects the coarsening of her
       character.

3. Conclusion
    Topic sentence: All details in the story,
    particularly the setting, are focused on the
    character of Mathilde.
```

The *conclusion* may be a summary of the body; it may evaluate the main idea; it may briefly suggest further points of discussion; or it may be a reflection on the details of the body.

Use Your Outline When Developing Your Essay

The illustrative essay included in this book is organized according to the principles of the analytical sentence outline. To emphasize the shaping effect of this outline, the central idea, thesis sentence, and topic sentences are underlined. In your own writing, you can underline or italicize these "skeletal" sentences as a check on your organization. Unless your instructor requires such markings, however, remove them in your final drafts.

Illustrative Essay (First Draft)

The following illustrative essay is a first draft of the subject we have been developing. It follows our outline, and it includes details from the story in support of the various topics. It is by no means, however, as good a piece of writing as it could be. The draft omits a topic, some additional details, and some new insights that are included in the second draft, which follows later (pp. 57–61). It therefore reveals the need to make improvements through additional brainstorming and discovery-prewriting techniques.

James Deal   Deal 1

Professor Roberts

English 102

12 January 2011

How Setting in "The Necklace" Is Related

to the Character of Mathilde

1   In "The Necklace" Guy de Maupassant does not give

much detail about the setting. He does not even describe

the necklace itself, which is the central object in his

plot, but he says only that it is "superb" (9).

Deal 2

Rather, he uses the setting to reflect the character of the central figure, Mathilde Loisel.[*] All his details are presented to bring out her traits. Her character growth is related to her first apartment, her dream-life mansion rooms, and her attic flat.[†]

2 Details about her first apartment explain her dissatisfaction and depression. The walls are "drab," the furniture "threadbare," and the curtains "ugly" (6). There is only a simple country girl to do the housework. The tablecloth is not changed daily, and the best dinner dish is beef stew. Mathilde has no evening clothes, only a theater dress that she does not like. These details show her dissatisfaction about her life with her low-salaried husband.

3 Her dream-life images of wealth are like the apartment because they too make her unhappy. In her daydreams about life in a mansion, the rooms are large, filled with expensive furniture and bric-a-brac, and draped in silk. She imagines private rooms for intimate talks, and big dinners with delicacies like trout and quail. With dreams of such a rich home, she feels even more despair about her modest apartment on the Street of Martyrs in Paris.

[*]Central idea
[†]Thesis sentence

4   The attic flat reflects the coarsening of Mathilde's character. Maupassant emphasizes the burdens she endures to save money, such as mopping floors, cleaning greasy and encrusted pots and pans, taking out the garbage, and washing clothes and dishes by hand. This work makes her rough and coarse, a fact also shown by her giving up care of her hair and hands, wearing the cheapest dresses possible, haggling with local shopkeepers, and becoming loud and penny-pinching. If at the beginning she is delicate and attractive, at the end she is unpleasant and coarse.

5   Maupassant focuses everything in the story, including the setting, on the character of Mathilde. He does not add anything extra. Thus he says little about the big party scene, but emphasizes the necessary detail that Mathilde was a great "success" (9). It is this detail that brings out some of her early attractiveness and charm, despite her more usual frustration and unhappiness. Thus in "The Necklace," Maupassant uses setting as a means to his end—the story of Mathilde and her unnecessary sacrifice.

6

COMPLETING THE ESSAY: DEVELOPING AND STRENGTHENING YOUR ESSAY THROUGH REVISION

After finishing your first draft, like this one, you may wonder what more you can do. Things may seem to be complete as they are, and that's it. You have read the work several times, have used discovering and brainstorming techniques to establish ideas to write about, have made an outline of your ideas, and have written a full draft. How can you do better?

The best way to begin is to observe that a common mistake writers make when writing about literature is to do no more than retell a story or summarize an idea. Retelling a story shows only that you have read it, not that you have thought about it. Writing a good essay requires you to arrange a pattern of argument and thought.

Make Your Own Arrangement of Details and Ideas

One way to escape the trap of summarizing stories and to set up a pattern of development is to stress your own order when referring to parts of a work. Rearrange details to suit your own central idea or argument. It is often important to write first about the conclusion or middle. Should you find that you have followed the chronological order of the work instead of stressing your own order, you can use one of the preliminary writing techniques to figure out new ways to connect your materials. The principle is that you should introduce details about the work *only* to support the points you wish to make. Details for the sake of detail alone are unnecessary.

Use Details from the Work as Evidence to Support Your Argument

When you write, you are like a detective, using clues as evidence for building a case, or a lawyer citing evidence to support an argument. Your goal is to convince your readers of your knowledge and the reasonableness of your conclusions. It is vital to use evidence convincingly so that your readers can follow your ideas. Let us look briefly at two drafts of a new example to see how writing can be improved by the pointed use of details. These are from drafts of an essay about the character of Mathilde, from Maupassant's "The Necklace."

Paragraph 1	Paragraph 2
The major flaw of Mathilde's character is that she seems to be isolated, locked away from other people. She and her husband do not talk to each other much, except about external things. He speaks about his liking for beef stew, and she states that she cannot accept the big invitation because she has no nice dresses. Once she gets the dress, she complains because she has no jewelry. Even when borrowing the necklace from Jeanne Forrestier, she does not say much. When she and her husband discover that the necklace is lost, they simply go over the details, and Loisel dictates a letter of explanation,	The major flaw of Mathilde's character is that she is withdrawn and uncommunicative, apparently unwilling or unable to form an intimate relationship. For example, she and her husband do not talk to each other much, except about external things such as his taste for beef stew and her lack of a party dress and jewelry. With such an uncommunicative marriage, one might suppose that she would be more open with her close friend, Jeanne Forrestier, but Mathilde does not say much even to her. This flaw hurts her greatly, because if she were more open she might have explained the loss and avoided the horrible

which Mathilde writes in her own hand. Even when she meets Jeanne on the Champs-Elysées, Mathilde does not say a great deal about her life but only goes through enough details about the loss and replacement of the necklace to make Jeanne exclaim about the needlessness of the ten-year sacrifice.	sacrifice. This lack of openness, along with her self-indulgent dreaminess, is her biggest defect.

A comparison of these paragraphs shows that the first has more words than the second (156 compared to 119 [computer count]) but that it is more appropriate for a rough than a final draft because the writer does little more than retell the story. Paragraph 1 is cluttered with details that do not support any conclusions. If you try to find what it says about Maupassant's actual use of Mathilde's solitary traits in "The Necklace," you will get little help. The writer needs to revise the paragraph by eliminating details that do not support the central idea.

On the other hand, the details in paragraph 2 actually do support the declared topic. Phrases such as "for example," "with such," and "this lack" show that the writer of paragraph 2 has assumed that the audience knows the story and now wants to read an argument in support of a particular interpretation. Paragraph 2 therefore guides readers by connecting the details to the topic. It uses these details as evidence, *not* as a retelling of actions. By contrast, paragraph 1 recounts a number of relevant actions *but does not connect them to the topic*. More details, of course, could have been added to the second paragraph, but they are unnecessary because the paragraph develops the argument with the details used. Good writing has many qualities, but one of the most important is shown in a comparison of the two paragraphs: *In good writing, no details are included unless they are used as supporting evidence in a pattern of thought and argument.*

Always Keep to Your Point; Stick to It Tenaciously

To show another distinction between first- and second-draft writing, let us consider a third example. The following unrevised paragraph, in which the writer assumes an audience that is interested in the relationship of economics to literature, is drawn from an essay about the idea of economic determinism in Maupassant's "The Necklace." In this paragraph the writer is trying to argue the point that economic circumstances underlie a number of incidents in the story. The idea is to assert that Mathilde's difficulties result not from her character traits but rather from her financial restrictions.

> <u>More important than chance in governing life is the idea that people are controlled by economic circumstances</u>. Mathilde, as is shown at the story's opening, is born poor. Therefore she doesn't get the right doors opened for her, and she settles down to marriage with a minor clerk, Loisel. With a vivid imagination and a burning desire for luxury, seeming to be born only for a life of ease and wealth, she finds that her poor home brings out her daydreams of expensive surroundings. She taunts her husband when he brings the big invitation, because she does not have a suitable (that is, "expensive") dress. Once she gets the dress it is jewelry she lacks, and she borrows that and loses it. The loss of the necklace means great trouble because it forces the Loisels to borrow heavily and to struggle financially for ten years.

This paragraph begins with an effective topic sentence, indicating that the writer has a good plan. The remaining part, however, shows how easily writers can be diverted from their objective. The flaw is that the material of the paragraph, while accurate, is not clearly connected to the topic. Once the second sentence is under way, the paragraph gets lost in a retelling of events, and the promising topic sentence is forgotten. The paragraph therefore shows that the use of detail alone will not support an intended meaning or argument. *As a writer, you must do the connecting yourself, and make sure that all relationships are explicitly clear.* This point cannot be overstressed.

How might the faulty paragraph be improved? The best way is to remind the reader again and again of the topic and to use examples from the text in support. If you are analyzing *point of view*, for example, you should keep connecting your material to the speaker, or narrator, and the same applies to topics such as character, idea, or setting. According to this principle, we might revise the paragraph on economic determinism in "The Necklace" as follows. (Parts of sentences stressing the relationship of the examples to the topic sentence are underlined.)

> More important than chance in governing life is the idea that people are controlled by economic circumstances. <u>As illustration</u>, the speaker begins by emphasizing that Mathilde, the main character, is born poor. Therefore she doesn't get the right doors opened for her, and she settles down to marriage with a minor clerk, Loisel. <u>In keeping with the idea</u>, her vivid imagination and burning desire for luxury feed on her weakness of character as she feels deep unhappiness and depression because of the contrast between her daydreams of expensive surroundings and the poor home she actually has. <u>These strained economic circumstances</u> inhibit her relationship with her husband, and she taunts him when he brings the big invitation because she does not have a suitable (that is, "expensive") dress. As a merging of her unrealistic dream life with actual reality, <u>her borrowing of the necklace suggests the impossibility of overcoming economic restrictions</u>. In the context of the idea, the ten-year sacrifice to pay for the lost necklace <u>demonstrates that being poor keeps people down, destroying their dreams and their hopes for a better life</u>.

The paragraph now successfully develops the argument promised by the topic sentence. While it has also been lengthened, the length has been caused not by inessential detail, but by phrases and sentences that give form and direction. You might object that if you lengthened all your paragraphs in this way, your essays would grow too bulky.

The answer is to reduce the number of major points and paragraphs, on the theory that *it is better to develop a few topics pointedly than to develop many pointlessly*. Revising for the purpose of strengthening central and topic ideas requires that you either throw out some topics or else incorporate them as subpoints in the topics you keep. To control your writing in this way can result only in improvement.

Try to Be Original

In everything you write, now and in the future, you should always try to be original. You might claim that originality is impossible because you are writing about someone else's work. "The author has said everything," might be the argument, "and therefore I can do little more than follow the story." This claim rests on the mistaken assumption that you have no choice in selecting material and no opportunity to have individual thoughts and make original contributions.

But you do have choices and opportunities to be original. You really do. One obvious area of originality is the development and formulation of your central idea. For example, a natural first response to "The Necklace" is: "The story is about a woman who loses a borrowed necklace and endures hardship to help pay for it." But this response does not promise an argument because it refers only to events in the story and not to any idea. You can point the sentence toward an argument, however, if you call the hardship "needless." Just this word alone demands that you explain the differences between needed and unneeded hardships, and your application of these differences to the heroine's plight would produce an original essay. Even better and more original insights could result if the topic of the budding essay were to connect the dreamy, withdrawn traits of the main character to her misfortunes. A resulting central idea might be: "People create their own difficulties." Such an argument would require you to define not only the personal, but also the representative nature of Mathilde's experiences, an avenue of exploration that could produce much in the way of a fresh, original essay about "The Necklace."

You can also develop your ability to treat your subject originally if you plan the body of the essay to build up to what you think is your most important and incisive idea. As examples of such planning, the following brief outline suggests how a central idea can be widened and expanded:

```
Argument: Mathilde Grows as a Character in "The Necklace"
1. She has normal daydreams about a better life.
2. In trying to make her daydreams seem real, she takes
   a risk but then loses.
3. She develops by facing her mistake and working hard
   to correct it.
```

The list shows how you can enlarge a subject if you treat your exemplifying details in an increasing order of importance. In this case, the order moves from Mathilde's habit of daydreaming to her growing strength of character. The pattern shows how you can meet two primary standards of excellence in writing—organization and growth.

Clearly, you should always try to develop your central idea or argument. Constantly adhere to your topic, and constantly develop it. Nurture it and make it grow. Admittedly, in a short essay you will be able to move only a short distance with an idea or argument, but you should never be satisfied to leave the idea exactly where you found it. To the degree that you can learn to develop your ideas, you will receive recognition for increasingly original writing.

Write with Specific Readers as Your Intended Audience

Whenever you write, you must decide how much detail to discuss. Usually you base this decision on your judgment of your readers. For example, if you assume that they have not read the work, you will need to include a short summary as background. Otherwise, they may not understand your argument.

Consider, too, whether your readers have any special interests or concerns. If they are particularly interested in politics, sociology, religion, or psychology, for example, you may need to select and develop your materials along one of these lines.

Your instructor will let you know who your audience is. Usually, it will be your instructor or your fellow students. They will be familiar with the work and will not expect you to retell a story or summarize an argument. Rather, they will want you to explain and interpret the work in the light of your main assertions about it. Thus, you can omit details that do not exemplify and support your argument, even if these details are important parts of the work. What you write should always be based on your developing idea together with your assessment of your readers.

The Use of Verb Tenses in the Discussion of Literary Works

Literary works spring to life with each and every reading. You may thus assume that everything happening takes place in the present, and when writing about literature you should use the *present tense of verbs*. It is correct to say, "Mathilde and her husband *work* and *economize* [not *worked* and *economized*] for ten years to pay off the 18,000-franc loan they *take out* [not *took out*] to pay for the lost necklace."

When you consider an author's ideas, the present tense is also proper, on the principle that the words of an author are just as alive and current today (and tomorrow) as they were at the moment of writing, even if this same author might have been dead for hundreds or even thousands of years.

Because it is incorrect to shift tenses inappropriately, you may encounter a problem when you refer to actions that have occurred prior to the time of the main action. An instance is Ambrose Bierce's short story "An Occurrence at Owl Creek Bridge," in which the main character, a Southern gentleman during the Civil War, is about to be hanged by Union soldiers because he had tried to sabotage a strategically important bridge. The story emphasizes the relationship between cause (the attempted sabotage, occurring in the past) and effect (the punishment, occurring in the present). In discussing such a narrative it is important to keep details in order, and thus you can introduce the past tense as long as you make the relationship clear between past and present, as in this example: "Farquhar *is actually hanged* [present tense] by the Union soldiers. But his perceptions *turn him* [present tense] toward the past, and his final thoughts *dwell* [present tense] on the life and happiness he *knew* [past tense] at his own home with his dearest wife." This intermingling of past and present tenses is correct because it corresponds to the pattern of time brought out in the story.

A problem also arises when you introduce historical or biographical details about a work or author. It is appropriate to use the *past tense* for such details if they genuinely do belong to the past. Thus it is correct to state, "William Shakespeare *lived* from 1564 to 1616," or that "Shakespeare *wrote* his tragedy *Hamlet* in about 1601." It is also permissible to mix past and present tenses when you are treating historical facts about a literary work and are considering it as a living text. Of prime importance is to keep things straight. Here is an example showing how past tenses (in bold) and present tenses (in italic) may be used when appropriate:

> Because *Hamlet* **was** first **performed** in about 1601, Shakespeare most probably **wrote** it shortly before this time. In the play, a tragedy, Shakespeare *treats* an act of vengeance, but more importantly he *demonstrates* the difficulty of ever learning the exact truth. The hero, Prince Hamlet, *is* the focus of this difficulty, for the task of revenge *is assigned* to him by the Ghost of his father. Although the Ghost *claims* that his brother, Claudius, *is* his murderer, Hamlet *is at first not able to verify this claim.*

Here, the historical details are in the past tense, while all details about the play *Hamlet*, including Shakespeare as the creating author whose ideas and words are still alive, are in the present.

As a general principle, you will be right most of the time if you use the present tense exclusively for literary details and the past tense for historical details. *When in doubt, however, always consult your instructor.*

Use Exact, Comprehensive, and Forceful Language

In addition to being original, organized, and well developed, the best writing is exact, comprehensive, and forceful. At any stage of the composition process, you should try to correct and improve your earliest sentences and paragraphs, which usually need to be rethought, reworded, and rearranged.

Try to make your sentences meaningful. First, ask yourself whether your sentences mean what you really intend, or whether you can make them more exact and therefore stronger. For example, consider these two sentences from essays about "The Necklace":

1. It seems as though the main character's dreams of luxury cause her to respond as she does in the story.

2. This incident, although it may seem trivial or unimportant, has substantial significance in the creation of the story. Meaning that the incident that occurred is essentially what the story is all about.

These sentences are inexact and vague, and therefore unhelpful. Neither of them goes anywhere. Sentence 1 is satisfactory up to the verb *cause*, but then it falls apart because the writer has lost sight of an argumentative or thematic purpose. It would be better to describe what the response *is* rather than to say nothing more than that some kind of response *exists*. To make the sentence more exact, we might try the following revision:

Mathilde's dreams of luxury make her dissatisfied with her own possessions, and therefore she goes beyond her financial means to attend the big party.

With this revision, the writer could readily go on to consider the relationship of the early part of the story to the later parts. Without the revision, it is not clear where the writer might go.

Sentence 2 is vague because the writer has lost all contact with the main thread of argument. If we adopt the principle of trying to be exact, however, we can create more meaning and more promise:

The accidental loss of the necklace, which is trivial though costly, supports the narrator's claim that major turns in life are produced not by earthshaking events but rather by minor ones.

In addition to working for exactness, try to make sentences—all sentences, but particularly thesis and topic sentences—complete and comprehensive. Consider the following sentence:

```
The idea in "The Necklace" is that Mathilde and her
husband work hard to pay for the lost necklace.
```

Although this sentence promises to describe an idea, it does no more than state the story's major action. It needs additional rethinking and rephrasing to make it more comprehensive, as in these two revisions:

```
1. In "The Necklace" Maupassant brings out the
   importance of overcoming mistakes through hard work
   and responsibility.

2. Maupassant's surprise ending in "The Necklace"
   symbolizes the need for always being truthful.
```

Both new sentences are connected to the action described by the original phrasing, "Mathilde and her husband work hard to pay for the lost necklace," although they point toward differing treatments. The first sentence concerns the virtue shown by the Loisels in their sacrifice. Because the second sentence includes the word *symbolizes*, an essay stemming from it would stress the Loisels' mistake in not confessing the loss. In dealing with the symbolic meaning of their failure, an essay developed along the lines of the second sentence would focus on the negative sides of their characters, and an essay developed from the first sentence would stress their positive sides. Both of the revised sentences, therefore, are more comprehensive than the original sentence and thus would help a writer get on the track toward a thoughtful and analytical essay.

Of course, creating fine sentences is never easy, but as a mode of improvement, you might use some self-testing mechanisms:

- *For story materials.* Always relate the materials to a point or argument. Do not say simply, "Mathilde works constantly for ten years to help pay off the debt." Instead, blend the material into a point, like this: "Mathilde's ten-year effort shows her resolution to overcome the horror of indebtedness," or "Mathilde's ten-year effort brings out her strength of character."

- *For responses and impressions.* Do not state simply, "The story's ending leaves a definite impression." What are you telling your readers by writing a sentence like this? They want to know what your impression is, and therefore you need to describe it as exactly as you can, as in the following: "The story's ending surprises and makes the reader sympathetic to the major character," or "The story's ending strikes the reader with the idea that life is unpredictable and unfair."
- *For ideas.* Make the idea clear and direct. Do not write, "Mathilde lives in a poor household," but rather refer to the story to bring out an idea, as follows: "Mathilde's story shows that being poor hurts a person's quality of life."
- *For critical commentary.* Do not be satisfied with a statement such as, "I found 'The Necklace' interesting." All right, the story is interesting, but what does that tell us? Instead, try to describe *what* was interesting and *why* it was interesting, as in this sentence: "The Necklace' is interesting because it shows how chance and bad luck may disrupt or even destroy people's lives."

Good writing begins with attempts, like these, to rephrase sentences to make them really say something. If you always name and pin down descriptions, responses, and judgments, no matter how difficult the task seems, your sentences will be strong and forceful because you will be making them exact and comprehensive.

Illustrative essay (Improved Draft)

If you refer again to the first draft of the essay about Maupassant's use of setting to illustrate Mathilde's character (pp. 42–44), you might notice that several parts of the draft need extensive reworking and revising. For example, paragraph 2 contains a series of short, unconnected comments, and the last sentence of that paragraph implies that Mathilde's dissatisfaction relates mainly to her husband rather than to her general circumstances. Paragraph 4 focuses too much on Mathilde's coarseness and not enough on her sacrifice and cooperation. The first draft also ignores the fact that the story ends in another location, the fashionable Parisian street the Champs-Elysées, where Maupassant continues to demonstrate the nature of Mathilde's character. Finally, there is not enough support in this draft for the contention (in paragraph 5) that everything in the story is related to the character of Mathilde.

To discover how these issues can be more fully considered, the following revision of the earlier draft creates more introductory detail, includes an additional paragraph, and reshapes each of the paragraphs to stress the relationship of the central idea or argument to the topics of the various paragraphs. Within the limits of a short assignment, the essay illustrates all the principles of organization and unity that we have been discussing here.

James Deal   Deal 1

Professor Roberts

English 102

18 February 2011

        How Maupassant Uses Setting in "The Necklace"

                to Show the Character of Mathilde

1   In "The Necklace," Guy de Maupassant uses setting

      to reflect the character and development of the main

      character, Mathilde Loisel.[*] As a result, his setting is

      not particularly vivid or detailed. He does not even

      describe the ill-fated necklace—the central object in

      the story—but states only that it is "superb" (9). In

      fact, he includes descriptions of setting only if they

      illuminate qualities about Mathilde. Her changing

[*]Central idea.

Deal 2

character can be connected to the first apartment, the
dream-life mansion rooms, the attic flat, and a
fashionable public street.[†]

2   Details about the modest apartment of the Loisels on
the Street of Martyrs indicate Mathilde's peevish lack
of adjustment to life. Though everything is serviceable,
she is unhappy with the "drab" walls, "threadbare"
furniture, and "ugly" curtains (6). She has domestic
help, but she wants more servants than the simple
country girl who does the household chores in the
apartment. Her embarrassment and dissatisfaction are
shown by details of her irregularly cleaned tablecloth
and the plain and inelegant beef stew that her husband
adores. Even her best theater dress, which is appropriate
for apartment life but which is inappropriate for more
wealthy surroundings, makes her unhappy. All these
details of the apartment establish that Mathilde's major
trait at the story's beginning is maladjustment. She
therefore seems unpleasant and unsympathetic.

3   Like the real-life apartment, the impossibly wealthy
setting of her daydreams about owning a mansion
strengthens her unhappiness and her avoidance of
reality. All the rooms of her fantasies are large and

†Thesis sentence.

Deal 3

expensive, draped in silk and filled with nothing but the best furniture and bric-a-brac. Maupassant gives us the following description of her dream world:

> She imagined a gourmet-prepared main course carried on the most exquisite trays and served on the most beautiful dishes, with whispered gallantries that she would hear with a sphinx-like smile as she dined on the pink meat of a trout or the delicate wing of a quail. (6)

With such impossible dreams, her despair is complete. Ironically, this despair, together with her inability to live with reality, brings about her undoing. It makes her agree to borrow the necklace (which is just as unreal as her daydreams of wealth), and losing the necklace drives her into the reality of giving up her apartment and moving into the attic flat.

4   <u>Also ironically, the attic flat is related to the coarsening of her character while at the same time it brings out her best qualities of hard work and honesty</u>. Maupassant emphasizes the drudgery of the work Mathilde endures to maintain the flat, such as walking up many stairs, washing floors with large buckets of water, cleaning greasy and encrusted pots and pans, taking out

Deal 4

the garbage, washing clothes by hand, and haggling
loudly with local shopkeepers. All this reflects her
coarsening and loss of sensibility, also shown by her
giving up hair and hand care and by wearing cheap
dresses. The work she performs, however, makes her
"heroic" (12). As she cooperates to help her husband pay
back the loans, her dreams of a mansion fade, and all
she has left is the memory of her triumphant appearance
at the Minister of Education's party. Thus the attic
flat brings out her physical change for the worse at the
same time that it also brings out her psychological
change for the better.

5   Her walk on the Champs-Elysées illustrates another
combination of traits—self-indulgence and frankness. The
Champs-Elysées is the most fashionable street in Paris,
and her walk to it is similar to her earlier indulgences
in her daydreams of upper-class wealth. But it is on this
street where she meets Jeanne, and it is her frankness
in confessing to Jeanne that makes her completely
honest. While the walk thus serves as the occasion for
the story's concluding surprise and irony, Mathilde's
being on the Champs-Elysées is totally in character, in
keeping with her earlier reveries about luxury.

6   Other details in the story also have a similar
bearing on Mathilde's character. For example, the story

Deal 5

presents little detail about the party scene beyond the statement that Mathilde is a great "success" (9)—a judgment that shows her ability to shine if given the chance. After she and Loisel accept the fact that the necklace cannot be found, Maupassant includes details about the Parisian streets, about the visits to loan sharks, and about the jewelry shops in order to bring out Mathilde's sense of honesty and pride as she "heroically" prepares to live her new life of poverty. Thus, in "The Necklace," Maupassant uses setting to highlight Mathilde's maladjustment, her needless misfortune, her loss of youth and beauty, and finally her growth as a responsible human being.

Deal 6

Work Cited

Maupassant, Guy de. "The Necklace." *What Every Student Should Know About Writing About Literature*. Ed. Edgar V. Roberts. New York: Pearson, 2012. 5-14. Print.

You will find here several improvements to the first draft. The language of paragraph 2 has been revised to show more clearly the inappropriateness of Mathilde's dissatisfaction. In paragraph 3, the irony of the story is brought out, and the writer has connected the details to the central idea in a richer pattern of ideas, showing the effects of Mathilde's despair. Paragraph 5—new in the improved draft—includes additional details about how Mathilde's walk on the Champs-Elysées is related to her character. In paragraph 6, the fact that Mathilde is able "to shine" at the dinner party is interpreted according to the central idea. Finally, the conclusion is now much more specific, summarizing the change in Mathilde's character rather than simply stating that the setting reveals "her needless misfortune." In short, the second draft reflects the complexity of "The Necklace" better than the first draft. Because the writer has revised the first-draft ideas about the story, the final essay is tightly structured, insightful, and forceful.

A Summary of Guidelines

To sum up, follow these guidelines whenever you write about a story or any kind of literature:

- Do not simply retell the story or summarize the work. Bring in story materials only when you can use them as support for your central idea or argument.
- Throughout your essay, keep reminding your reader of your central idea.
- Within each paragraph, make sure that you stress your topic idea.
- Develop your subject. Make it bigger than it was when you began.
- Always make your statements exact, comprehensive, and forceful.
- And this bears repeating: Do not simply retell the story or summarize the work.

7

A Short Guide to Using Quotations and Making References in Essays about Literature

In establishing evidence for the points you make in your essays, paragraphs, and essay examinations, you constantly need to refer to various parts of stories, plays, and poems. You also need to include shorter and longer quotations, and to keep the time sequences straight within the works you are writing about. In addition, you may need to refer to biographical and historical details that have a bearing on the work or works you are studying. So that your own writing may flow as accurately and naturally as possible, you must be able to integrate these references and distinctions of time clearly and easily.

Integrate Passages and Ideas into Your Essay

Your essays should reflect your own thought as you study and analyze the characteristics, ideas, and qualities of an author's work. In a typical discussion of literature, you constantly need to introduce brief summaries, quotations, general interpretations, observations, and independent applications of everything you are discussing. It is not easy to keep these various elements integrated and to keep confusion from arising.

Distinguish Your Own Thoughts from Those of Your Author

A serious problem is that it is often hard for your reader to figure out when *your* ideas have stopped and your *author's* have begun. You must therefore arrange your sentences to make the distinctions clear, but you must also blend your materials so that your reader can follow you easily. Let us see an example of how such problems may be handled. Here, the writer is discussing the poem "Dover Beach," by the English Victorian poet Matthew Arnold (1822–1888). The passage moves from reference to Arnold's ideas to the essay writer's independent application of the ideas.

> [1] In his poem "Dover Beach," Arnold states that in past times religious faith was accepted as absolute truth. [2] To symbolize this idea he refers to the ocean, which surrounds all land, and the surf, which constantly rushes onto the Earth's shores. [3] According to this symbolism, religious ideas are as vast as the ocean and as regular as the surf, and these ideas at one time constantly and irresistibly replenished people's lives. [4] Arnold's symbol of the flowing ocean changes, however, to a symbol of the ebbing ocean, thus illustrating his idea that belief and religious certainty were falling away. [5] It is this personal sense of spiritual emptiness that Arnold is associating with his own times, because what he describes, in keeping with the symbolism, is that in the present time the "drear" shoreline has been left vacant by the "melancholy long withdrawing roar" of retreat and reduction (lines 25–27).

This specimen paragraph combines but also separates paraphrase, interpretation, and quotation, and it thereby eliminates any possible confusion about the origin of the ideas and also about who is saying what. In the first three sentences the writer uses the phrases "Arnold states," "To symbolize this idea," and "According to this symbolism," to show clearly that interpretation is to follow. Although the fourth sentence marks a new direction of Arnold's ideas, it continues to separate restatement from interpretation. The fifth sentence indicates, through the phrase "in keeping with the symbolism," what seems to the writer to be the main idea of "Dover Beach."

Integrate Material by Using Quotation Marks

It is often necessary, and also interesting, to use short quotations from your author to illustrate and reinforce your ideas and interpretations. Here, the problem of separating your thoughts from the author's is solved by quotation marks. In such an internal quotation, you may treat prose and poetry in the same way. If a poetic quotation extends from the end of one line to the beginning of another, however, indicate the line break with a virgule (/), as in the following paragraph about the poem, "Lines Written in Early Spring," by the English Romantic poet William Wordsworth:

> In "Lines Written in Early Spring" Wordsworth
> describes a condition in which his speaker is united
> with the surrounding natural world. Nature is a
> combination of the "thousand blended notes" of joyful
> birds (line 1), the sights of "budding twigs" (17), and
> the "periwinkle" (10). In the exact words of the
> speaker, these "fair works" directly "link / The human
> soul that through me ran" (5-6).

As the example above shows, when creating parenthetical citations for poetry, use the line numbers of the poem. When citing short stories and novels, use the page number from the edition you are using. Since novels, short stories, and plays are often available in many editions, some instructors may prefer that you assume that your reader may have a text different from yours. Therefore, you will need to provide the information necessary for finding the exact location, regardless of the edition of the text that you use. For example, if you are quoting from a play with act, scene, and line numbers, refer to Act (Arabic numeral), scene (Arabic numeral), and line number (Arabic numeral), in parentheses following the quotation, as in (3.1.33). Use periods to separate these numbers:

> Hamlet's famous soliloquy makes use of vivid martial
> imagery in its early lines when it states that "The
> slings and arrows of outrageous fortune, / Or to take
> arms against a sea of troubles" (3.1.59–60).

This citation reveals that in any edition of *Hamlet*, the reader could find this line in Act 3, Scene 1, lines 59–60.

Many other professors will prefer that you use your parenthetical references to direct readers to the page where the material appears in the text you are using. The reader can then be assumed to use the works cited list to find the exact edition. The important thing about referring to parts of novels, short stories, and plays is that you be clear and exact. The guidance offered here will cover most situations, but complications and exceptions will occur. When they do, always ask your instructor what to do and what systems of reference to use.

Blend Quotations into Your Own Sentences

The use of internal quotations still creates the problem of blending materials, however, for quotations should never be brought in unless you prepare your reader for them in some way.

Do not, for example, use quotations in the following manner:

> Wordsworth states that his woodland grove is filled
> with the sounds of birds, the sights of flowers, and the
> feeling of the light wind, making for the thought that
> creatures of the natural world take pleasure in life.
> "The birds around me hopped and played."

This abrupt quotation throws the reader off balance because it is not blended into the previous sentence. It is necessary to prepare the reader to move from your discussion to the quotation, as in the following revision:

> Wordsworth claims that his woodland scene is made
> joyful by the surrounding flowers and the gentle breeze,
> causing his speaker, who states that "The birds around
> me hopped and played" (line 13), to conclude that the
> natural world has resulted from a "holy plan" (22)
> created by Nature.

Here, the quotation is made an actual part of the sentence. This sort of blending is satisfactory, provided that the quotation is brief.

Indenting and Blocking Long Quotations

You can follow a general rule for incorporating quotations in your writing: Do not quote within a sentence any passage longer than four typed lines of prose or more than three lines of poetry (but consult your instructor, for the allowable number of lines may vary). Quotations of greater length demand so much separate attention that they interfere with your own sentence. It is possible, but not desirable, to conclude one of your sentences with a quotation, but you should never make an extensive quotation in the *middle* of a sentence. By the time you finish such an unwieldy sentence, your reader will have forgotten how it began—and how can that be clear writing? When your quotation is long, you should make a point of introducing it and setting it off separately as a block.

The physical layout of block quotations should be this: Start the block quotation on a new line. Double-space the quotation (like the rest of your essay), and indent it five spaces from your left margin to distinguish it from your own writing. You might use fewer spaces for longer lines of poetry, but the standard should always be to create a balanced, neat page. After the quotation, begin a new line, and resume your own discourse. Here is another passage from an essay about Wordsworth's "Lines Written in Early Spring":

> In "Lines Written in Early Spring" Wordsworth develops an idea that the world of nature is linked directly to the moral human consciousness. He speaks of no religious systems or books of moral values. Instead, he derives his ideas directly from his experience, assuming that the world was made for the joy of the living creatures in it, including human beings ("man"), and that anyone disturbing that power of joy is violating "Nature's holy plan" (line 22) itself. Wordsworth's moral criticism, in other words, is derived from his faith in the integrity of creation:

> > If this belief from heaven be sent,
> >
> > If such be Nature's holy plan,

```
Have I not reason to lament

What man has made of man? (21—24)
```

```
The concept that morality and life are joined is the

most interesting and engaging aspect of the poem. It

seems to encourage a live-and-let-live attitude toward

others, however, not an active program of direct

outreach and help.
```

When quoting lines of poetry, always remember to quote them *as lines.* Do not run them together as though they were continuous prose. When you create block quotations, such as in the preceding example, you do *not* need quotation marks.

Use Ellipses to Show Omissions

Whether your quotation is long or short, you will often need to change some of the material in it to conform to your own sentence requirements. You might wish to omit something from the quotation that is not essential to your point or to the flow of your sentence. Indicate such omissions with ellipses (three spaced periods), as follows (from an essay about Eudora Welty's short story "A Worn Path"):

```
Welty introduces Phoenix as an aging and impoverished

but also lovely and delicate woman. Phoenix's dress,

which reaches to "her shoe tops," is protected by a

"long apron of bleached sugar sacks" (314). Her skin has

"a pattern all its own of numberless branching wrinkles,

. . . but a golden color ran underneath" (314).

Nevertheless, her hair is shaped "in the frailest of

ringlets, . . . with an odor like copper" (314).
```

If your quotation is very brief, however, do not use ellipses because they might be more distracting than helpful. For example, *do not* use ellipses in a quotation like this:

> Keats asserts that ". . . a thing of beauty . . ." always gives joy (line 1).

Instead, make your quotation without the ellipses:

Keats asserts that "a thing of beauty" always gives joy (line 1).

Use Square Brackets to Enclose Words That You Add within Quotations

If you add words to integrate a quotation into your own train of discourse, or to explain words that may seem obscure, put square brackets around them, as in the following passage:

> In "Lines Written in Early Spring," Wordsworth refers to a past experience of extreme happiness, in which Nature seemed to "link / The human soul that through . . . [him] ran" (lines 5-6). He is describing a state of mystical awareness in which "pleasant thoughts / Bring [him] sad thoughts," and make him "lament" moral and political cruelty (2–8).

Do Not Overquote

A word of caution: *Do not use too many quotations.* You will be judged on your own thought and on the continuity and development of your own essay. It is tempting to include many quotations on the theory that you need to use examples from the text to illustrate and support your ideas. Naturally, it is important to introduce examples, but realize that too many quotations can disturb the flow of your own thought. If your essay consists of many illustrations linked together by no more than your introductory sentences, how much thought have you actually put into it? Try, therefore, to create your own discussion, using appropriate examples to connect your thought to the work you are analyzing.

Appendix

DOCUMENTING YOUR WORK IN MLA STYLE

The previous section explored how to correctly quote from works of literature in your essays. When writing about literature, the literature itself is considered a primary source. For some assignments, your instructor may ask you to consult secondary sources—sources that analyze or comment on literature. If you are writing using secondary sources, it is necessary and essential to acknowledge—to *document*—all sources from which you have quoted, paraphrased, or summarized factual and interpretive information. In order to avoid being challenged for plagiarism, this point cannot be overemphasized. As the means of documentation, various reference systems use parenthetical references, footnotes, or endnotes. Whatever system is used, documentation almost always includes a carefully prepared bibliography, or list of works cited.

Plagiarism: An Embarrassing but Vital Subject— and a Danger to Be Overcome

When you are using sources as the substance of many of the details in your essay, you run the risk of plagiarism—using the words and ideas of other writers without their consent and without acknowledgment. Recognizing the source means being clear about the identity of other authors, together with the name or names of the works from which one gets details and ideas. When there is no recognition, readers, and the intellectual world generally, are deceived. They assume that the material they are reading is the original work and the intellectual possession of the writer. When there is no recognition, the plagiarizing author is committing intellectual theft.

This is no small matter. In the world of publications, many people who have committed plagiarism have suffered irreparable damage to their credibility and reputations as writers and authorities. Some well-known writers have found it hard, if not impossible, to continue their careers, and all because of the wide knowledge of their plagiarism. It does not end there. A plagiarist might be open to legal actions, and might, if the situation is grave enough, be required to supply financial restitution to the author or authors whose work has been illegally appropriated. In schools and colleges, students who plagiarize may face academic discipline. Often the discipline is a failure for the course, but it might also include suspension and expulsion.

In this section, we will review the major reference system for use in a literary paper. Parenthetical references, preferred by the Modern Language Association (MLA) since 1984, are described in the *MLA Handbook for Writers of Research Papers*, 7th ed., 2009. We explore this style of documentation in detail below and provide an extensive list of sample works cited listings. *Always consult your instructor regarding which documentation system to use.*

Refer to Works Parenthetically as You Draw Details from Them

Within the text of your essay, use parentheses in referring to works from which you are using facts and conclusions. This parenthetical citation system is recommended in the *MLA Handbook* (pp. 213–32), and its guiding principle is to provide documentation without asking readers to interrupt their reading to find footnotes or endnotes. Readers wanting to see the complete reference can easily find it in your list of works cited. With this system, you incorporate the author's last name and the relevant page number or numbers directly, whenever possible, into the body of your essay. If the author's name is mentioned in your discussion, you need to give only the page number or numbers in parentheses.

Here are two examples, from a critical study of another author, the eighteenth-century poet Alexander Pope:

> ```
> Alexander Pope believed in the idea that the universe
> is a whole, a totally unified body, which provides a
> "viable benevolent system for the salvation of everyone
> who does good" (Kallich 24).
> ```

> ```
> Martin Kallich draws attention to Alexander Pope's
> belief in the idea that the universe is a whole, a
> totally unified body, which provides a "viable benevolent
> system for the salvation of everyone who does good" (24).
> ```

Include All the Works You Have Used in a List of Works Cited (Bibliography)

The key to any reference system is a carefully prepared list of works cited, which is included at the end of the essay. "Works cited" means exactly that; the list should include just those books and articles you have actually used in your essay. If your instructor requires, however, you can extend your concluding list to be a complete bibliography both of works cited and of works consulted but not actually used. Always, always, always, follow your instructor's directions.

The list of works cited should include the following information, in each entry, in the form indicated.

For a Book

- The author's name: last name first, followed by first name and middle name or initial. Period.
- The title, italicized. Period.
- The city of publication (not state or nation), colon; publisher (easily recognized abbreviations or key words can be used unless they seem awkward or strange; see the *MLA Handbook,* pp. 233–257), comma; year of publication. Period.
- The medium of publication (Print, Web, etc.). Period.

For an Article

- The author's name: last name first, followed by first name and middle name or initial. Period.
- The title of the article in quotation marks. Period.
- The title of the journal or periodical, italicized, followed by the volume and issue numbers in Arabic (not Roman) numbers with no punctuation, then the year of publication within parentheses. Colon. For a daily paper or weekly magazine, omit the parentheses and cite the date in the British style followed by a colon (day, month, year, as in 2 Feb. 2010). Inclusive page numbers (without any preceding p. or pp.). Period.
- The medium of publication (Print, Web, DVD, etc.). Period.
- If your article was obtained through a database, include the database name. If your article was obtained electronically, either through a database or on the Internet, include the date you visited the site. Period.

For a Web Publication

- The author's name: last name first, followed by first name and middle name or initial. Period.
- The title of work/site. Italicize if the document is independent or use quotation marks if it is a part of a larger work.
- Web site's name, italicized (if this is different than above).
- Publisher. Comma. Publication Date. Use "n.d." if no publication date is available.
- The medium of publication (Print, Web, etc.). Period.
- The access date, meaning the date you viewed the site. Period.
- The URL (uniform resource locator). The MLA specifies that the URLs should no longer accompany works cited entries unless the URL is essential to locating the site. If you determine that the URL is necessary, include the full address (be absolutely accurate in reproducing the URL) and place angle brackets (< >) before and after. Period. (Note: when a URL continues from one line to the next, break it *before* punctuation.)

The works you are citing should be listed alphabetically according to the last names of authors, with unsigned articles included in the list alphabetically by titles. Bibliographical lists are begun at the left margin, with subsequent lines in a five space hanging indentation, so that the key locating word—the author's last name or the first title word of an unsigned article—can be easily seen. The entire works cited section should be double spaced, as should the rest of your essay. Many unpredictable and complex combinations, including ways to describe works of art, musical or other performances, and films, are detailed extensively in the *MLA Handbook* (pp. 123–212).

Sample MLA Works Cited Entries
Book by One Author

Fitzgerald, F. Scott. *The Great Gatsby*. New York:

    Scribner, 1925. Print.

Book with No Author Listed

The Pictorial History of the Guitar. New York: Random,

    1992. Print.

Book by Two (or Three) Authors

Clemens, Samuel L., and Charles Dudley Warner. *The Gilded*

    Age: A Tale of Today. Hartford: American, 1874.

    Print.

Book by Four or More Authors

Guerin, Wilfred L., Earle Labor, Lee Morgan, Jeanne C.

    Reesman, and John R. Willingham. *A Handbook of*

    Critical Approaches to Literature. New York: Oxford

    UP, 2004. Print.

or

Guerin, Wilfred L., et al. *A Handbook of Critical Approaches to Literature*. New York: Oxford UP, 2004. Print.

Two Books by the Same Author

Reynolds, David S. *Beneath the American Renaissance*. Cambridge: Harvard UP, 1988. Print.

———. *Walt Whitman's America: A Cultural Biography*. New York: Knopf, 1995. Print.

Book with an Editor

Scharnhorst, Gary, ed. *Selected Letters of Bret Harte*. Norman: U of Oklahoma P, 1997. Print.

Book with an Author and an Editor

De Quille, Dan. *The Fighting Horse of the Stanislaus*. Ed. Lawrence I. Berkove. Iowa City: U of Iowa P, 1990. Print.

Translated Book

Cervantes Saavedra, Miguel de. *Don Quixote de la Mancha*. Trans. Charles Jarvis. New York: Oxford UP, 1999. Print.

Literary Work in an Anthology

Chopin, Kate. "The Storm." *Fiction 100: An Anthology of Short Fiction*. Ed. James H. Pickering. 12th ed. Upper Saddle River: Pearson, 2010. 256–61. Print.

Introduction, Preface, Foreword, or Afterword in a Book

Pryse, Marjorie. Introduction. *The Country of the Pointed Firs and Other Stories*. By Sarah Orne Jewett. New York: Norton, 1981. v–xix. Print.

Article in a Reference Book

Gerber, Phillip. "Naturalism." *The Encyclopedia of American Literature*. Ed. Steven Serafin. New York: Continuum, 1999. 808–09. Print.

Article in a Journal

Kruse, Horst. "The Motif of the Flattened Corpse." *Studies in American Humor* 3.4 (1997): 47–53. Print.

Book Review

Bird, John. Rev. of *The Singular Mark Twain*, by Fred Kaplan. *Mark Twain Annual* 2.1 (2004): 57–61. Print.

Article in a Newspaper

Albom, Mitch. "Longing for Another Slice of Dorm Pizza." *Detroit Free Press* 3 April 2005: C1. Print.

Editorial

"Death Penalty Debate Finally Produces Useful Result." Editorial. *USA Today* 22 June 2005: A15. Print.

Article in a Magazine

McDermott, John R. "The Famous Moustache That Was." *Life*

    20 Dec. 1968: 53–56. Print.

Lecture

Kaston Tange, Andrea. "The Importance of American

    Literature." Literature 100 class lecture. Eastern

    Michigan University, 5 Nov. 2010. Lecture.

E-Mail

Henderson, Elisabeth. Message to the author. 25 Feb. 2010.

    E-mail.

Interview for Which You Did the Interviewing

Stipe, Michael. Personal interview. 10 Nov. 2010.

Film

Napoleon Dynamite. Dir. Jared Hess. Fox Searchlight, 2004.

    DVD.

Television Program

"The Parking Garage." *Seinfeld*. NBC. WDIV, Detroit, 23

    Jul. 1994. Television.

Online Book with Print Information

Dickens, Charles. *David Copperfield*. New York, P. F. Collier,

    1917. *Bartleby Archive*, 1999. Web. 25 Mar. 2010.

Online Book Without Print Information

Shakespeare, William. *Hamlet*. c. 1601. *Project Gutenberg*.

Web. 25 Mar. 2008.

Journal Article on the Web

Hewlett, Beth L., and Christa Ehmann Powers. "How Do You

Ground Your Training? Sharing the Principles and

Processes of Preparing Educators for Online Writing

Instruction." *Kairos* 10.1 (2005): n.p. Web. 10 May

2010.

Journal Article in a Scholarly Database

Yates, Norris W. "The Doubt and Faith of John Updike."

College English 26.6 (1995): 469–474. *JSTOR*. Web. 12

May 2010.

Magazine Article on the Web

Jones, Kenneth. "Bill Gates and Steve Jobs Sing and Dance

in New Musical, Nerds, Already a Hit in NYM."

Playbill.com. 20 Sept. 2005. Web. 25 Mar. 2011.

Artwork on the Web

Leonardo da Vinci. *Mona Lisa*. Louvre, Paris. n.d. Web. 12

Dec. 2010.

Posting to a Discussion List

McElhearn, Kirk. "J. S. Bach: Oxford Composer Companion [A

    review]." Online posting. *Alternative Music*, J. S.

    Bach. Google Groups,

    1 Dec. 2000. Web. 24 Apr. 2010.

Professional Site

NobelMuseum. The Nobel Foundation, n.d. Web. 25 Mar. 2008.

Personal Site (with URL)

Barrett, Dan. *The Gentle Giant Home Page*. 19 Feb. 2008.

    Web. 25 Mar. 2010. <www.blazemonger.com/GG

    /index.html>.

ADDITIONAL TITLES IN THE **WESSKA**
(WHAT EVERY STUDENT SHOULD KNOW ABOUT…) SERIES:

- *What Every Student Should Know About Avoiding Plagiarism* (ISBN 0-321-44689-5)

- *What Every Student Should Know About Citing Sources with APA Documentation* (ISBN 0-205-79581-1)

- *What Every Student Should Know About Citing Sources with MLA Documentation* (ISBN 0-205-71511-7)

- *What Every Student Should Know About Reading Maps, Figures, Photographs, and More* (ISBN 0-205-50543-0)

- *What Every Student Should Know About Using a Handbook* (ISBN 0-205-56384-8)

- *What Every Student Should Know About Writing Across the Curriculum* (ISBN 0-205-58913-8).

- *What Every Student Should Know About Creating Portfolios* (ISBN 0-205-57250-2)

- *What Every Student Should Know About Practicing Peer Review* (ISBN 0-321-44848-0)

- *What Every Student Should Know About Preparing Effective Oral Presentations* (ISBN 0-205-50545-7)

- *What Every Student Should Know About Study Skills* (ISBN 0-321-44736-0)

- *What Every Student Should Know About Procrastination* (ISBN 0-205-58211-7)

- *What Every Student Should Know About Writing About World Literature* (ISBN 0-205-21166-6)